CONTENTS

SUSAN L. LINGO

200+ ACTIVITIES FOR CHILDREN'S MINISTRY

7/13/05

Standard PUBLISHING

CINCINNATI, OHIO

Dedication
Show me your ways, O Lord, teach me your paths;
guide me in your truth and teach me.
Psalm 25:4, 5

200+ Activities for Children's Ministry
©1999, 2003 Susan L. Lingo

Published by The Standard Publishing Company, Cincinnati, Ohio 45231. A division of Standex International Corporation.

Credits
Produced by Susan L. Lingo, Bright Ideas Books™
Illustrated by Liz Howe
Cover design by Liz Howe

09 08 07 06 05 04   10 9 8 7 6 5 4 3 2
ISBN 0-7847-1332-4
Printed in the United States of America

INTRODUCTION

Classroom teachers have a real juggling act!

Bible lessons, crafts, games, devotions, snacks, prayers, songs, bulletin boards, Scripture and worship ideas—whew! So much to manage and maintain, even more to teach and guide. Where can a busy teacher find enough ideas to keep the juggling act from tumbling down? In the pages of *200+ Activities for Children's Ministry!*

Here are over two hundred can't-miss ideas, lively lesson-boosters, snappy activities, and organizational helps all in one book. *200+ Activities for Children's Ministry* is divided into eight sections:

- **Creative Crafts**
- **Great Games**
- **Goodies Galore**
- **Prayer & Worship**
- **Devotions & Object Lessons**
- **Super Seasonals**
- **Awesome Organization**
- **SOS for the Substitute**

Each section is loaded with fresh ideas that are as fun for kids as they are friendly for teachers. And scattered throughout every section, you'll discover loads of Whatcha Know! boxes that contain helpful hints, ingenious insights, and terrific teaching tips. In addition, each section of *200+ Activities for Children's Ministry* has its own mini introduction to provide an overview and solid backdrop for what to expect in the section.

Crafts and games, worship ideas, lively devotions, snacks, and classroom checklists—you'll find them all in *200+ Activities for Children's Ministry*. This is the definitive teacher handbook of help, the one book you'll turn to over and over for every classroom concern, each classroom nook and need. And there's even a color-coded retrieval system to help you find just the section you're searching for in a snap! So what are you waiting for? Hop into any of these great classroom resources and...use them now!

How to Use the Color-Coded Retrieval Tabs

200+ Activities for Children's Ministry makes finding your favorite sections of the book as easy as 1-2-3!

1. Photocopy on cardstock the set of tabs below.
2. Color each tab a different color, then cut the tabs out.
3. Tape the tabs to the edges of the corresponding section title pages in a staggered pattern like dividers in a notebook.

CRAFTS	GAMES	GOODIES	PRAYER & WORSHIP
DEVOTIONS	SEASONAL IDEAS	ORGANIZATION TIPS	SOS for the SUBSTITUTE

CREATIVE CRAFTS

Clever cutlery, key verse key chains, tin can candles, prayer trees, and much more to delight and stretch kids' imaginations!

A Bit of Background

"Crafts are the best part of Sunday school!"
"I feel proud when I finish a cool craft project all by myself!"

Ever hear comments like these echoed by the kids in your class? That's because craft time is a favorite part of any children's program.

Crafts can turn an otherwise dull lesson into an unforgettable adventure with concrete reminders to carry home. Look for ways to integrate craft projects into your lessons by reinforcing Bible stories, devotions—even prayers. And don't be worried about how your kids' crafts may look or if they'll turn out, because the craft projects included in *200+ Activities for Children's Ministry* are easy-to-do and process-oriented rather than product-oriented. In other words, kids have the freedom to make their own projects look individual and unique—just as God created kids to be!

Consider making a craft cache to keep frequently used supplies at your fingertips for instant projects. Decorate a medium-sized box with colorful wrapping paper or festive Con-Tact paper. Include the following items in your craft cache and be sure to replace them when needed.

- ☐ markers & crayons
- ☐ scissors
- ☐ glue & clear tape
- ☐ cotton balls
- ☐ cotton swabs
- ☐ paper plates
- ☐ paper lunch sacks

- ☐ craft feathers
- ☐ ribbon & lace
- ☐ yarn & twine
- ☐ colored paper
- ☐ tissue paper
- ☐ small sponges
- ☐ sequins & glitter

Remember to try crafts ahead of time to become familiar with the process and to have an idea of the time the project will take. And remember also to have fun while encouraging your kids' sense of creativity and imagination!

Here are a few extra-helpful tips and hints to get you started:

✀ **Make lightning-quick paint shirts by cutting holes for arms and heads in paper grocery bags.**

✀ **Use a plastic ice scraper and hot soapy water to remove dried glue and paste from laminated tabletops.**

✀ **A bit of rubbing alcohol will remove most marker ink or paint from laminated tabletops or tile floors.**

COOL CLAY-WARE

Clever cutlery reminds kids of the importance of "devouring" God's Word!

Whatcha Need: You'll need clear spray shellac, colorful self-hardening clay, and a set of inexpensive metal flatware for each child. Secondhand stores have plenty of mismatched flatware you can pick up for a song!

Whatcha Do: Show children how to roll balls of different-colored clay into ¼-inch thick ropes. Pinch two ropes together at the top, then wind and twist the ropes around the handles of the flatware. Completely cover the entire length of each flatware handle. Be sure to securely pinch the ends together. As children work, discuss how learning God's Word is like being fed nutritious food. Remind children of the importance of learning to devour God's Word by themselves—just as they learned to feed themselves. When the clay hardens, spray it with clear shellac. Tell children to enjoy eating with their new utensils but to towel dry them after each washing.

KEY VERSE KEY CHAINS

Here are shiny reminders that God's Word is the key to our lives!

Whatcha Need: You'll need Bibles, 2-by-1-inch strips of white paper, fine-tipped felt pens, glue, acrylic paints, glitter glue, and one key chain and Formica chip for each child. Formica-chip samples with holes drilled in the ends are free at most building or decorating centers.

Whatcha Do: Set out the craft materials and let each child choose a favorite Formica chip. Then hand each child a slip of paper and a pen. Let children work in pairs to look up their favorite Scripture verses as each person chooses a verse to write on the slip of paper. Glue the verse to the Formica chip, then attach the key chain. If you want, add tiny touches of paint and glitter glue.

As kids work, discuss the importance of God's Word and how it helps us every day. When the Key Verse Key Chains are done, let children read their verses aloud and tell why they selected them. Encourage children to keep the chains attached to something they'll see often, such as backpacks, shoelaces, or coat zippers.

PICTURE-PERFECT PUZZLE

Fun reminders that God's will is no puzzle—it's perfect!

Whatcha Need: You'll need old jigsaw puzzles, Tacky craft glue, and one small plastic picture frame for each child. Have children bring in photographs of themselves.

Whatcha Do: Invite children to choose picture frames and place their pictures inside the frames. Then have children glue puzzle pieces around the frames. As you work, talk about jigsaw puzzles and how we can't see the whole picture until all the pieces are in their correct places. Visit about God's will and how God has a perfect plan for every person. Point out that God's plan for us is no puzzle—that God knows every piece and where each one fits. Discuss why obeying God helps accomplish his will through us. Encourage children to set their picture puzzles in their rooms to remind them that God has a picture-perfect plan for their lives.

FLEX YOUR FAITH!
Colorful wire sculptures show how God helps us.

Whatcha Need: You'll need a heavy-duty stapler, colored markers, colored electrical wire in various gauges, scissors, and a 6-inch wooden square for each child. Ask an adult volunteer to cut the wooden squares ½-inch thick.

Whatcha Do: Before class, cut the wire into 8-inch lengths. Cut five to ten wires for each child. Invite each child to choose five to ten wires and a wooden base, then help children securely staple the wires to the bases. Have children bend, twist, and shape their wires into flexible sculptures. Visit about what it means to be flexible when we have worries or troubles. Discuss ways God helps us stay flexible, such as through prayer, faith, love, and trust. Challenge children to sculpt models that show how they feel knowing that God helps us. Help children write "God helps us flex our faith" on the wooden bases, then decorate them with colorful markers.

SWEET SPOONS
Tasty teaspoons are sweet reminders of God's Word.

Whatcha Need: You'll need a box of plastic spoons, plastic sandwich bags, curling ribbon, honey, waxed paper, paper plates, and fruit-flavored gelatin powder.

Whatcha Do: Spread waxed paper on a table. Pour the gelatin powder on paper plates. Hand each child two or three spoons. Show children how to dip the spoons in honey and then roll them in fruit-flavored gelatin. Set the spoons on waxed paper to dry. As the spoons dry, read aloud Psalm 119:103 and visit about what makes God's Word sweet. Point out that just as honey is sweet and good for us, so is God's Word. When the spoons are dry, slip the rounded spoon ends in plastic bags and tie them with ribbons. Tell children they can be licked as suckers or given to adults to stir into their tea or coffee.

Whatcha Know!

Turn this creative craft into a super service project for senior citizens. Prepare sets of three spoons for each plastic sack. Tie the sacks with curled ribbon and attach cards with Psalm 119:103 and directions for how to sweeten coffee or tea written on them.

TRINITY PRETZEL SWAGS

Weaving three-ringed pretzels teaches kids about the Trinity.

Whatcha Need: You'll need a bag of large three-ringed pretzels, scissors, Tacky craft glue, and ribbons in 1-inch and ½-inch widths.

Whatcha Do: Hand each child a 2-foot length of 1-inch-wide ribbon and five pretzels (two to munch and three to weave). Show children how to weave the ribbon in and out of the pretzel rings as in the illustration. Glue the excess ribbon on each end to the backs of the pretzel swags. Use narrower ribbon to tie bows, then glue them to the ends of the swag as hangers. As you work, explain that just as pretzels have three rings that are joined to make one pretzel, God, Jesus, and the Holy Spirit are joined to form the Trinity. Also point out that the pretzel swags have three pretzels joined into one swag. Have children hang their Trinity Pretzel Swags on the wall to remind them that God's love is joined in the Trinity.

GLITTER-FLIES

These sparkly butterflies herald springtime.

Whatcha Need: You'll need a Bible, waxed paper, white paper, pencils, Tacky craft glue, glitter, and cookie sheets or sturdy cardboard.

Whatcha Know!

For bright springtime colors, stir powdered tempera paint into the glue before making your Glitter-Flies.

Whatcha Do: Spread the waxed paper on cookie sheets or sturdy cardboard. Have children draw simple butterfly outlines on white paper, then slide their papers under the waxed paper. Drizzle thick Tacky glue around the butterfly outlines, then sprinkle the glue with lots of glitter. Read 2 Corinthians 5:17 aloud and ask children how butterflies are like new creations in the springtime. Have children tell in what ways we're new creations when we love Jesus. Dry the Glitter-Flies for several days, then peel them from the waxed paper and use fishing line to suspend them in windows or from the ceiling.

GO TELL 'EM POUCH

A pouch full of fun tracts to give friends.

Whatcha Need: You'll need an old wallpaper book, scissors, rubber bands, markers, paper, and a stapler.

Whatcha Do: Have each child cut a page from the wallpaper book and fold the sheet in half. Staple the side edges together to make a rectangular pouch. Decorate the front of the pouch with markers. Help children staple two rubber bands to the top back edge of the pouch. The rubber bands will allow the pouches to slide onto belts or bicycle handlebars. Have children brainstorm things they could tell others about Jesus, then write the sentences on a sheet of paper. Make a photocopy of the paper for each child. Cut apart the sentences and place the slips of paper in the Go Tell 'Em Pouches. Challenge children to hand their tracts to friends, family, and others they meet to tell them about Jesus.

THE APPLE OF HIS HEART
Beautiful apple crafts remind children of God's love.

Whatcha Need: You'll need red delicious apples, twine, and scissors. Before class, cut the apples vertically into ¼-inch slices and rub them with lemon juice to keep them from turning brown. Place the apple slices on a cookie sheet and dry them for about 24 hours in a 225-degree oven. Turn the slices several times during the drying process. When the apple slices are dry, use a sharp pencil to punch two holes in opposite sides of each apple slice. Prepare four apple slices for each child. Cut a 3-foot piece of twine for each child.

Whatcha Do: Hand each child a piece of twine and four dried apple slices. Have children thread the twine in and out of the holes on the apple slices as shown in the illustration. Tie the excess twine on each side in a bow. As you work, point out how the apple slices look like hearts. Ask children why God's love is so special and how we can tell God we love him. Tell children to hang their heart-shaped apple crafts in a place to remind them of God's special love for us.

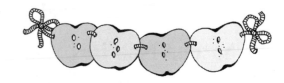

GOLDEN LEAVES
Lovely leaves make this a perfect autumn craft idea.

Whatcha Need: You'll need pressed autumn leaves, craft glue, water, waxed paper, glitter, cotton swabs, scissors, and self-adhesive magnetic strip. Thin the craft glue with a bit of water in a bowl.

Whatcha Do: Spread waxed paper on a table. Be sure the leaves are pressed flat. Invite each child to choose a leaf. Use cotton swabs to spread thinned glue over the veins of each leaf. Sprinkle glitter on the glue and let leaves dry overnight. Spread glue on the backs of the leaves and allow them to dry. Cut a ½-inch piece of magnetic tape to stick to the back of each leaf. Then use the glittery leaves to hold memos, Scripture verses, or special notes about God's goodness at harvesttime! Use this idea as a fund-raiser and have children sell their shiny creations to buy a needy family food for Thanksgiving.

TIN CAN CANDLES
Older children enjoy making these unusual candleholders.

Whatcha Need: You'll need clean metal cans, hammers, various sized nails, markers, and votive candles. Remove can labels and be sure the cans are clean and free of rough edges.

Whatcha Do: Hand each child a can and a marker. Have children trace a simple design on one side of the can, such as a cross, heart, star, flower, or dove shape. Show each child how to hold the can with his knees and gently tap a nail to make a small hole along the outline of the shape. Continue punching small holes along the outline at ½-inch intervals. Repeat the process on the other sides of the cans. As you work, explain that long ago churches used candles as light. Tin-punch candleholders made the candle light especially pretty and decorated the church in a nice way. When the cans are complete, place a votive candle in each holder. Tell children to ask an adult to light their candles as dinner table decorations. You may wish to present the candles to the minister to use during a church service.

PRAYER TREES

These terrific trees remind kids to pray.

Whatcha Need: You'll need large plastic cups, florists' clay, colored slips of paper, tape, pencils, ribbon, scissors, glitter glue, Easter grass or dried moss, and a tall branched twig for each child.

Whatcha Do: Hand each child a cup, a twig, and a lump of florists' clay. Have children push the lumps of clay into the bottoms of the cups, then push the twigs into clay. Next, fill the cup with Easter grass or dried moss. Tie ribbon bows to the branches, then decorate the cups and twigs with glitter glue. As the crafts dry, visit about the importance of praying for others. Ask what kinds of prayers we can pray on behalf of other people. Then give each child several slips of colored paper and have her write a prayer request on each slip. Tape a ribbon loop to each slip as a hanger. Ask children to exchange the prayer requests with friends, then hang the paper slips on their Prayer Trees. Encourage children to pray for each need every day for a week.

PUFF PUPPETS

Darling puppets help tell Bible stories.

Whatcha Need: You'll need polyester fiberfill, rubber bands, scissors, old nylon hosiery, sturdy sticks or twigs, Tacky craft glue, and a variety of craft scraps, including felt scraps, feathers, cotton balls, buttons, and sequins.

Whatcha Do: Cut a 5-inch length of hosiery for each puppet. Have children wrap rubber bands around the tops of the hosiery pieces, then stuff the hosiery with fiberfill until they're plump. Wrap another rubber band around the bottom of each puppet head, then poke a stick or twig up through the base. Use felt scraps and other decorative touches to add hair, hats, headbands, floppy ears, beards, or other features. Make animals, birds, and people for a whole cast of characters! Let children form groups and retell a favorite Bible story or passage using their Puff Puppets.

 # TAP-TAP TINS
Young children will be proud of these lovely tins.

Whatcha Need: You'll need sturdy aluminum pie tins, nails, small hammers or screwdrivers, Tacky craft glue, scissors, lace, and ribbon.

Whatcha Do: Ask several adult volunteers to help with this fun craft. Hand each child a nail and an aluminum pie tin. Help children use small hammers or screwdriver handles to tap nails into the backs of the pie tins to make holes in the shape of a cross. Tap the nails in, then pull them out to make holes. As you work, ask children who the cross reminds us of and remind children that Jesus loves each of us. Place the nails and tools out of reach when you're finished. Have children spread glue around the rims of the pie tins. Stick lace to the glue so that it extends outward from the edges of the tins. Then let children glue bows to the bottoms of the tins. Tell children to hang their Tap-Tap Tins on the wall to remind them of Jesus and his great love.

> ## Whatcha Know!
>
> Young children grow weary of paper crafts. Offer exciting grown-up projects to keep their interest high.

 # SWEET CENTERPIECE
A holiday centerpiece children will be pleased to make.

Whatcha Need: You'll need tape, wide ribbon, scissors, and one long taper candle and six candy canes for each child.

Whatcha Do: Have children work in pairs. To make each centerpiece, begin by taping an upside-down candy cane to a candle. Continue taping candy canes around the candle at ½-inch intervals. When you're finished, the crook of the candy canes should sit level on a table with the candle extending upward as in the illustration. Tie a bow around the center of the centerpiece. Tell children to have an adult light the candle. A new candle may be added by gently untaping then retaping the candy canes in place.

ARK-MOBILE

Young children can easily make this mobile.

Whatcha Need: You'll need colorful markers, tape, Tacky craft glue, fishing line, brown paper, scissors, and one box of animal crackers for each child. Cut five 10-inch lengths of fishing line for each child.

Whatcha Do: Give each child a box of animal crackers. Have children empty their animal crackers on the table and separate the whole animals from the broken pieces. Tell children they may nibble the broken pieces as they work. Color the animals with markers, then glue two animal crackers back-to-back with fishing line between them.

As you work, retell the Bible story of Noah's ark and how God sent the animals two-by-two to ride in the ark. Set the animals aside to dry. Tape brown paper to the cracker boxes and then color the "arks" with markers. Suspend the animal crackers from the arks by taping the ends of the fishing line to the bottoms of the boxes. Finally, tape a 3-foot length of fishing line to the top of each ark, then suspend the arks from the ceiling.

SWAT-THAT-FLY PAINTINGS

An outside summer craft kids will love.

Whatcha Need: You'll need a roll of white shelf paper, paper plates with tempera paints on them, raisins, and one flyswatter for each child.

Whatcha Know!
Turn these unique pictures into game boards. Let children take turns tossing raisin bugs and trying to make bulls-eyes by landing on flyswatter prints.

Whatcha Do: Roll out a 4-foot length of white paper for each child. Anchor the paper to grass by poking sticks through it or to a sidewalk using stones. Let children scatter raisin "bugs" on their papers. Show kids how to lightly dip their flyswatters in paint, then swat the bugs on their papers. Encourage children to use different colors of paint to create bright designs. Let the pictures dry, then dispose of any painted raisins that haven't stuck to the papers.

FROG-JOGGERS

Here are hoppity-fun reminders of God's power.

Whatcha Need: You'll need egg cartons, 2-foot lengths of string, scissors, green markers, glue, and construction paper.

Whatcha Do: Cut apart the individual egg cups from each egg carton. Hand each child an egg cup and a 2-foot piece of string. Then invite children to color their egg-cup frogs green. Add brown freckles, faces, and webbed feet made from green construction paper. Help children poke holes in the tops of their paper frogs, then thread the string up through the holes. Tie knots inside the egg cups to keep the string from pulling through. When children quickly lift the strings, their frogs will hippity-hop. Use the frogs to retell the Bible story of how God sent frogs to Egypt when his people were held captive. Remind children of God's amazing and miraculous power and how God can help us hop over worries and troubles. Then take your frogs for a "frog-jog" around the church or playground area.

ANGEL TREAT BAGS

These holiday treats are as fun to eat as they are to make.

Whatcha Need: You'll need wrapped candies, rubber bands, Tacky craft glue, small Styrofoam balls, scissors, ribbon, and 2-foot lengths of aluminum foil or tissue paper.

Whatcha Do: To make each angel, lay a 2-foot piece of aluminum foil or tissue paper on the floor. Place a small handful of wrapped candies in the center. Bring the short ends together, then gather the sides in toward the center as in the illustration. Pinch and secure with a rubber band, then tie a ribbon around the rubber band. Spread the foil or tissue paper outward above the ribbon to make a nest, then glue a small Styrofoam ball head in the center. Let the angels dry. If you're using tissue paper, add a dot of glue on each side to keep the candies from escaping. Finally, add ribbon loops to hang on Christmas trees or make extras to hand out at a children's hospital.

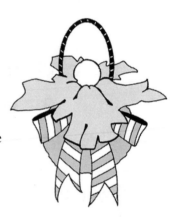

20 BATIK BANNERS

Children love this colorful two-part craft.

Whatcha Need: You'll need 12-inch squares of white cotton, rubber cement, newspapers, aluminum foil, paintbrushes, and neon tempera paints.

Whatcha Do: Cover a table with newspapers. Hand each child a square of white cotton. Invite children to dribble or brush thick lines of rubber cement over their fabric in designs. Encourage children to make designs that symbolize their love for Jesus, such as hearts, sunshine, the cross, or doves.

Let the fabric dry for several hours or overnight. Then let children lay their fabric squares on pieces of foil and paint them with neon tempera paints. The rubber cement will resist the paint and leave tactile designs! Hang the dry banners in a hallway for everyone to enjoy or sew them together to make a lovely wall hanging for the church sanctuary.

JONAH'S SEA-FARI

This clever craft is a guaranteed kid-pleaser!

Whatcha Need: You'll need Styrofoam meat trays, permanent markers, fishing line, scissors, rocks or seashells, toothpicks, water, and one tall clear plastic cup for each child.

Whatcha Do: Let children draw and color small fish on a meat tray, then carefully cut them out. As you work, retell the Bible story of Jonah and the great fish. Point out how God saved Jonah when Jonah repented and obeyed God. Then use a toothpick to gently punch a hole at the bottom of each fish. Thread fishing line through the hole and tie it to the fish, then tie the other end to a rock or seashell. Place a rock or seashell with a fish attached at the bottom of each plastic cup. Slowly pour water into the cup and the fish will float—just as if it's swimming in the sea!

TWINKLY STARS

What a perfect VBS craft!

Whatcha Need: You'll need chenille wires, water, borax (available at grocery stores), food coloring, pencils, 6-inch pieces of string, and a wide-mouthed glass or jar for each child.

Whatcha Do: Have an adult fill each jar or glass with boiling water. Stir in 3 tablespoons of borax, one at a time, until powder begins to settle on the bottom of each jar. Stir in food coloring to create a dark tint. Let children bend their chenille wires into star shapes. Tie string to each star and the other ends to pencils. Rest the pencils on top of the jars and dangle the stars in the liquid. Set the jars aside for overnight. The next day, glittery borax crystals will have formed on the stars. Carefully remove the stars and hang them to dry. Then hang them in windows as lovely twinkly sun-catchers!

FANCY FLOWER PRINTS

These unique prints really get noticed.

Whatcha Need: You'll need squares of unbleached muslin, hammers, paper grocery sacks, and an assortment of fresh flowers and leaves.

Whatcha Do: Place paper grocery sacks on a hard surface such as a sidewalk or tile floor. Have children spread their muslin squares on the paper and sprinkle a variety of fresh leaves and flowers on one half of the fabric. Fold over the fabric and feel where the outlines of the flowers and leaves are, then pound on top of the items being sure to go all the way to the edges. When the colors from the flowers and leaves have bled through, open the fabric and scrape off any plant residue. There will be a mirror image of the plant life to frame or use as a pillow coverlet. Try pounding flowers and leaves onto paper for a different effect!

CONFETTI CANDLES

Remind older children that Jesus is the light of the world.

Whatcha Need: You'll need various colors of wax chips (available in craft stores), toothpicks, paper plates, an electric skillet, and one chunky 6-inch candle for each child.

Whatcha Do: Ask an adult volunteer to supervise using the electric skillet. Heat the skillet to medium. Place wax bits and toothpicks on a paper plate. Hand each child a paper plate and chunky candle. Show children how to stab a wax bit with a toothpick and carefully hold the wax chip on the electric skillet until it begins to melt. Quickly stick the wax chip to the side of the chunky candle, then carefully remove the toothpick. Continue melting and sticking wax chips to the candles.

As you work, ask children to tell reasons that Jesus is a light to the world. Tell children to have an adult light the candle at dinnertime. Then challenge children to offer a prayer thanking Jesus for being the light of the world.

> ## Whatcha Know!
>
> Use these lovely lights for Mother's Day gifts or for a special Easter centerpiece!

 # CHURCH SERVICE CRAFT

This cool craft is really a great gift for the entire church!

Whatcha Need: You'll need two very large clay pots, a very large clay pot base (that fits under a pot to gather water), florists' clay, spray shellac, tempera paints, and paintbrushes.

Whatcha Do: Take the pots and base outside with the craft supplies. Form three groups and hand each group either a clay pot or the base. Challenge each group to cooperatively paint the sides of its item with colorful flowers, birds, sunshine, clouds, and other outdoor pictures. As children paint, have them name their favorite parts of God's creation and explain why each is a favorite.

When the items are dry, spray them with clear shellac. Stack the pots as shown in the illustration, then place the clay base on top. Plug the hole in the base with plenty of waterproof florists' clay. Then fill the base with water to make a church garden birdbath or with seeds to make a bird feeder for everyone to enjoy!

HEARTS-ON-A-STRING

A "scent-sational" craft for Valentine's Day!

Whatcha Need: You'll need two cans of applesauce, 8 ounces of cinnamon, ⅔ cup white glue, a rolling pin, small heart-shaped cookie cutters, a mixing bowl, toothpicks, cooling racks, and 1-foot long pieces of twine. This is a two-day craft project, so plan ahead.

Whatcha Do: Mix the applesauce, cinnamon, and glue until they form a ball. Chill the dough ball at least half an hour. (It can be chilled overnight.) Sprinkle a bit of cinnamon on a table and roll the dough out to ¼-inch thickness. Have each child cut out at least three hearts. (This recipe makes about twenty-five 2-inch hearts.) Poke two holes side-by-side in the center of each heart, then place the hearts on a cooling rack to dry overnight. Thread the hearts on the twine and tie bows in the ends of the twine.

Whatcha Know!

Add drops of clove, cinnamon, or peppermint oil to modeling dough to make scented shapes and beads.

GREAT GAMES

Rowdy races, daring dodge ball, Bible games, and more team up for rib-tickling fun— and loads of cooperation and communication!

A Bit of Background

Hopscotch, tag, tug-of-war, charades, four-square—what was your favorite game as a child? Games come in such a variety of shapes and sizes, it may be hard to choose! From indoor to outdoor, cooperative to competitive, small group to individual relays and races, games are perennial favorites with kids of all ages. But games aren't just for fun—they're for learning too! Adding quality games to your children's programming offers kids the chance to

- increase communication skills,
- build community,
- solve problems,
- nurture teamwork and friendships,
- tame the wiggles, and
- learn about good sportsmanship.

Great games can help kids feel part of a team, part of a bigger group—just like their teamwork in Christ's body of believers! And many games can emphasize Christian values such as cooperation, kindness, helpfulness, obeying rules, and sharing.

Many teachers feel that cooperative games—games with no winners or losers—are the only kind of games for their children. But gentle competition need not be ignored or pushed away. Achieving the highest number of points isn't the only way to score a game. Look for innovative scoring that encourages kids instead of discouraging them, such as awarding points for endurance, style, imagination, kindness, or other quality traits. Older kids especially enjoy a bit of gentle competition and striving to be the best they can be.

Become familiar with the games in the Great Games section of *200+ Activities for Children's Ministry* and you'll be ready at a wiggle's notice for fun and frolic your kids will love!

Here are a few extra-helpful tips and hints to get you started:

✳ **Make beanbags in a snap by pouring uncooked rice or beans into socks, then knotting them at the ankles and cutting off any extra material.**

✳ **Use plastic tumblers as relay obstacles, pylons, for ball-tossers, or as bases. Try using tumblers as objects to pass in a relay!**

✳ **Plastic margarine lids make great Frisbees to toss and catch as well as bases for games such as kick ball and baseball.**

DANIEL'S DANGEROUS DEN
Guard "Daniel" from ferocious "lions."

Whatcha Need: You'll need a playground ball and several empty milk cartons.

Whatcha Know!

Use this quick 'n easy game to review the story of Daniel in the lions' den. If you're stuck for milk cartons, simply use old books or chalkboard erasers.

Whatcha Do: This game is similar to dodge ball. Choose several children to be lions. Have the rest of the children be angels. Form as many small groups of angels as there are milk carton "Daniels." Explain that the object of this game is for the lions to roll the playground ball and try to topple each milk carton while the angels guard the cartons by deflecting the ball and rolling it back at the lions. If a lion is tagged by the ball, she must sit down for the remainder of the game. If a carton is toppled, the angels guarding that carton move to help another group guard its carton. Continue until all the lions are tagged or all the milk cartons are toppled.

CLEAN YOUR CLOSET
This high-energy game gets the wiggles out.

Whatcha Need: You'll need masking tape and a variety of items such as paper wads, erasers, scarves, tennis balls, sponges, coasters, paper cups, cotton balls, and pillows. You'll need at least twenty items.

Whatcha Do: Place a masking tape line in the center of the play area and set an equal number of items on each side of the line. Form two groups and have each stand on one side of the line. Explain that this game is a lot like cleaning a closet or room—everything must be on the other side of the line before you call time. Tell kids they'll have 3 minutes to toss, slide, or roll their items to the other side of the center line. Call time after 3 minutes and count the number of items on each side. The side with the fewest number gets drinks first or chooses the next game.

Whatcha Know!

This game is great at family picnics! Use old paper cups to play, then toss them in the trash when you're finished!

TRIANGLE BALLOON-BLOW
Huff-n-puff and have loads of fun.

Whatcha Need: You'll need masking tape and balloons.

Whatcha Do: Mark off a 5-foot masking tape square on the floor. Make a masking tape X from corner to corner. Form four groups and have each stand in a triangle within the square. Explain that in this game, each group begins with 3 points and tries to blow the balloon into another team's

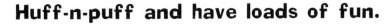

triangle. Groups may cooperatively blow the balloon—but no touching allowed! If the balloon touches the ground in a triangle, that group subtracts 1 point. Play until one group is out of points. Toss a balloon in the air to begin the game. After you've played several times, choose new groups and play with more than one balloon.

GIGGLE-N-GO
This zany game is strictly for grins.

Whatcha Need: You'll need a sheet of paper.

Whatcha Do: Choose one person to be the Gigglemeister and hand that player a sheet of paper. Have the Gigglemeister stand at one end of the room and line everyone else up at the opposite end. Explain that when the Gigglemeister drops the paper, everyone is to slowly walk forward while laughing. When the Gigglemeister picks up the paper, everyone must freeze—and no one must laugh or even smile. If the Gigglemeister catches someone moving or laughing, that person must go back to the starting place and begin again. Play until someone reaches the Gigglemeister and touches the paper. Then that person becomes the next Gigglemeister.

NOAH'S RAINBOW CATCH
Younger children will enjoy this outdoor game.

Whatcha Need: You'll need a roll of crepe paper and two twigs.

Whatcha Do: Unroll the crepe paper across the center of a grassy play area and use twigs to attach the crepe paper ends to the ground. Have children stand on one side of the crepe paper and think of a color of the rainbow they'd like to be. Then choose a child to be Noah. Have Noah stand on the crepe-paper rainbow and call out a color. All children with that color must try to run across the rainbow before being tagged by Noah. If they're tagged, they help Noah tag others. Continue calling out colors and running back and forth across the rainbow until everyone has been tagged.

CAPTURE THE ARK
Older kids love the challenge of this outdoor game.

Whatcha Need: You'll need two empty cereal boxes and two jump ropes.

Whatcha Do: Lay the jump ropes across the center of the playing area. Form two teams and have teams stand on opposite sides of the center line. Place one cereal box on each side about 30 feet from the center line. Explain that in this game players try to seize the cereal box "ark" from their opponent's side of the playing field. Players who are tagged by the other team must sit out for 3 minutes before they rejoin their team. Challenge the children to brainstorm game plans and to cooperate with other team members to capture the ark! The winning side gets to line up first for a drink of water.

COMET-BALL CATCH
Kids will love making these cool comets.

Whatcha Need: You'll need colored vinyl tape and one plastic trash bag and one old tennis ball for each child. If you can't find tennis balls, use pairs of old socks rolled into balls!

Whatcha Do: Have children form pairs and make their comet balls. To make a comet, slip a tennis ball into the corner of a trash bag. Twist the ends of the bag as you wind 6-inch strips of red, blue, green, and yellow colored tape around it. Then use the comet balls to play the following games.

✱ **Sally's Comet:** Form a circle with one child in the center. Toss the comet ball high as the center child calls out the name of someone in the circle. Have that child run in to catch the comet. If successful, he can call out the next name.

✱ **Comet Color-Call:** Have kids form pairs. Instruct partners to stand about 10 feet apart, decide which color to catch the comet on, then toss each other the comet balls. The partner closest to the correct color gets 1 point. Score 2 points for a bulls-eye!

✱ **Comet-Tail Twirl:** Play in groups of three. One person holds a comet ball by the tail and swings the ball around on the ground while the others try to jump over it. When someone misses a jump, she becomes the next twirler.

BOUNCE-ALONG
There's loads of cooperative fun in this zany game.

Whatcha Need: You'll need two of each of the following items: ball, bedsheet, plastic cup, pillow, shoe, small wooden block, and milk carton.

Whatcha Know!

Try this game at a family picnic and relay items to the trash. Fun cleanup in a snap!

Whatcha Do: Form two teams and have each team choose someone to be the tosser and someone to be the catcher. The rest of the team members will be bouncers. Place one of each of the items in a pile beside the tossers. Have the bouncers hold the edges of the bedsheet and stand about 5 feet from the tossers. Then position the catchers about 15 feet from the bouncers. Explain that in this zany game the tosser will toss an item onto the bedsheet. The bouncers will launch the item to the catcher who will set the items in a pile. If a toss or catch is missed, the item must be returned to the tosser and tossed again. The first team to successfully launch and catch all its items must sit down.

LITTLE LOST LAMB
Young children love this quiet seek-and-find game.

Whatcha Need: You'll need two scarves and a wind-up kitchen timer. Be sure the timer has a loud ticktock sound.

Whatcha Do: Have children kneel to form a large circle. Choose two children to be shepherds and use scarves to blindfold them. Wind up the lost lamb timer and place it somewhere in the circle. Explain that shepherds must crawl on their hands and knees to find the little lost sheep. When the lost sheep is found, have children clap and say, "He is found!" Then choose two new shepherds. Play until everyone has been a shepherd at least once. If you have a large group, use four scarves and have four shepherds search for the lost lamb.

> ## Whatcha Know!
>
> This game is a great follow-up to Jesus' parable of the Lost Sheep.

SCRIPTURE PASS
This classroom game helps kids learn Bible verses.

Whatcha Need: You'll need index cards and a pen.

Whatcha Do: Choose a Scripture verse to learn or review. Write each word of the verse on one index card. Have children sit in a circle and then choose one child to be the clapper and to sit in the center. When the clapper says "go," have kids begin passing the cards in different directions around the circle. When the clapper says "freeze," the cards must be read in their correct order. After several repetitions, children will be able to snap out the words! For a fun twist, pass the cards in different ways, such as under knees or behind backs, or pass the words to two verses at one time!

COOPERATIVE BOWLING
Fast fun with a little help from your friends.

Whatcha Need: You'll need masking tape, red and yellow tape, ten empty milk cartons, and several tennis balls or playground balls.

Whatcha Do: Place yellow tape around the center of five milk cartons and red tape around the centers of the other five. Stick a masking tape line down the center of your play area. Alternate the red and yellow milk cartons at equal intervals down the length of the line.

Have children form two groups and stand on opposite sides of the line about 15 feet from the cartons. Designate one team as the Reds and the other as the Yellows. Instruct children to find partners on their teams and decide who will roll the ball (rollers) and who will pick up the ball (lifters) for this first game. Have teams take turns rolling the balls back and forth and trying to bowl over their color milk cartons. Remind kids that only the lifters can pick up the balls and only the rollers may roll them! When one team's pins are all toppled, they score 1 point. Have partners switch roles and play again. Play until one team has 5 points.

CLOTHESPIN HANDSHAKE

This game is a great icebreaker for older kids.

Whatcha Need: You'll need twelve clothespins.

Whatcha Do: Form four groups of kids and have each group stand in a line. Have the first person in each line place three clothespins between his fingers as shown in the illustration. On "go," the first players turn and introduce themselves to the players behind them. Then they must shake hands with their new acquaintances and transfer the clothespins from finger to finger! If a clothespin drops, replace it and continue. The first line making the tricky clothespin handshake all the way to the end is the winner and may choose the next game.

PEANUT PASS
This is a game of cooperation and skill.

Whatcha Need: You'll need a bag of peanuts still in the shell.

Whatcha Do: Choose four players to be one team called the Innies. The rest of the children are the Outies and are to form a standing circle. Have one of the Innies stand inside the circle. The object of the game is for the rest of the Innies to pass three peanuts to the player in the center. The Outies try to block the passes by locking elbows, squatting low, or raising their arms. Continue play until all three peanuts are passed successfully to the player in the center. Choose new teams and play again. Then use the peanuts in these fun relays.

* Form four lines and have team members pass peanuts over their heads and under their knees from one end to the other and back again.

* Have team members do the crab walk to shuttle a pile of peanuts from one end of the room to the other. How can kids carry the peanuts? On their tummies!

STOP THAT POP!
This game's a perfect party-pleaser!

Whatcha Need: You'll need balloons and masking tape.

Whatcha Do: Have each child blow up and tie off a balloon. Hand each child a 2-foot length of masking tape. Instruct kids to stick one end of the tape securely to their balloons and the other end around their shoelaces or ankles. The object of the game? To try to hop and pop everyone else's balloons while guarding your own! For a variation, use string or yarn instead of masking tape and attach balloons to both feet of each player.

CATERPILLAR CRAWL
Kids of all ages love this wiggly-giggly relay.

Whatcha Need: No supplies required.

Whatcha Do: Designate a starting line and a finish line. Have children form groups of four or five, then line up behind the starting line. When you say "go," have the first person in line lie down on his tummy facing the finish line. Have the next person in line run to lie down in front so the first player can grab his ankles. Have the third person in line run to lie down at the front and so on. When all team members are lying on their tummies and holding the ankles of the person in front, the last person in line jumps up and runs to the front. Continue in this way until all caterpillars have reached the finish line. Play again, but choose new caterpillar teams.

NOAH'S RAINY-DAY RELAY
This bouncy game is a favorite with young children.

Whatcha Need: You'll need balloons and masking tape.

Whatcha Do: Blow up and tie off a balloon for each child. Use masking tape to mark starting and finish lines on the floor about 15 feet apart. Tell children that the finish line is the pretend ark and that they're going to be make-believe animals traveling to the ark. Line children up at the starting line and have them use their balloons to pretend to be the following animals:

Whatcha Know!

When you're done playing, let children tape construction-paper eyes, ears, mouths, trunks, and feet to their balloons to make ark animals.

- ✳ Kangaroos: place balloons between their knees and hop.

- ✳ Elephants: place balloons on their noses like trunks and walk.

- ✳ Ducks: place balloons between their ankles and waddle.

- ✳ Birds: flap their balloons as they fly.

- ✳ Frogs: bop their balloons up and down as they hop.

BIBLE ABC

A fast-paced classroom game for older children

Whatcha Need: You'll need a ball.

Whatcha Do: Have children form a standing circle. Decide which category from the Bible to play with, such as Bible books, places, foods, or names. Toss the ball to someone who can name a word beginning with A in the chosen category—for example, Abraham. Then toss the ball to another person, who must name a B word and so on.

If someone cannot answer, she may call on a lifesaver. If the lifesaver can name a correct word, play continues. If not, begin with a new category or skip that letter and look up a word to fill it in later as a class. When you've run out of biblical ideas, try naming breakfast cereals, types of cars, or animals.

BIBLE BOOK SNATCH

This is a fun way for kids to learn the books of the Bible.

Whatcha Need: You'll need masking tape and a Bible.

Whatcha Do: Place a 6-foot masking tape square on the floor and set the Bible in the center. Have children form four teams and have each team stand on a different line in the square. Assign New Testament Bible book names to kids, making sure at least two children from different teams have the same book name. For example, two children might be Matthew, two might be Mark, and so on.

When everyone has a Bible book, call out a book from the New Testament. Kids with that name rush to pick up the Bible. The first child to pick up the Bible has 15 seconds to locate that New Testament book and show it to the others. Teams score 2 points each time a correct Bible book is shown. Play until one team scores 6 points. Repeat the game, but assign new Bible book names or use books of the Old Testament.

SCRAMBLE CAR
This game is fast-paced indoor fun.

Whatcha Need: No supplies required.

Whatcha Do: Clear a playing area in the center of the floor. Have children form groups of four and sit on the floor in pretend cars with two in the front seat (driver and passenger) and one or two in the back seat (rear passengers). If there's a child without a car, she can be the first caller. Call out verbal driving instructions such as "left turn," "right turn," "put on the brakes," "passengers switch places," and "speed bump." Have children follow the directions or act out the motions. Whenever you call out "scramble car," have kids rush to form new cars and begin again. If your group is very large, try having buses with ten passengers each instead of cars.

CRAB SOCCER
Wear jeans for this silly soccer game.

Whatcha Need: You'll need a large playground ball and six plastic cups.

Whatcha Do: Scatter the plastic cups around the playing area at least 6 feet apart. Form two teams: the Blue Hermit Crabs and the Red Horseshoe Crabs. Have teams sit in the center of the playing area. Explain that in this game all players must do the crab walk as they try to use the ball to knock over plastic cups. If a Blue Hermit Crab team member knocks over a cup, he yells, "blue crab!" and scores 1 point. Red Horseshoe Crab members call out "red crab!" Play continues until all cups are toppled. Add the points scored and play until one team scores 12 points. The team with the most points lines up first for drinks.

GIFTS OF THE MAGI
Play this lively game outside on a sunny day.

Whatcha Need: You'll need two each of the following items: scarves, small boxes, and beanbags.

XX

Whatcha Do: Choose a starting place, then set pairs of objects (or gifts) according to the diagram. Have children form two teams and line up at the starting place. Choose someone to be the caller, then explain that the object of this game is for each team to collect one of every gift and make it back to the starting place. Have the caller give directions such as, "Take two giant steps" or "Walk backwards five paces." All children are to take the directed steps toward the gifts of their choice. (Everyone

XX   caller   XX

_____

starting
line

will be going in different directions!) When a gift is collected for a team, players must travel back to the starting place. They may pass or toss gifts to a fellow team member who may be further along. The first team with all the gifts and all players back at the starting place scores 3 points. Play until a team accumulates 12 points.

LEAPIN' LIZARDS!

Get things hopping with this fun game.

Whatcha Need: You'll need masking tape and a playground ball.

Whatcha Know!

Play a game of cooperative Leapin' Lizards by having lizards lock elbows as they leap over the ball.

Whatcha Do: Mark out a 10-foot masking tape square or circle on the floor. Choose two children to be rollers who stand outside and on opposite sides of the circle or square. Tell the rest of the children they are pretend lizards who must leap over the ball as it rolls at them. Have the rollers roll the ball quickly back and forth across the play area as the lizards leap and hop to avoid being tagged. When a lizard is tagged, he becomes a roller and helps tag out other lizards. Play until only one lizard is left. For more excitement, roll two or three balls simultaneously!

JUNK STORE

This crazy relay will have your kids hooting!

Whatcha Need: You'll need two identical piles of "junk." Include items such as pillows, sponges, hats, jackets, tennis balls, pennies, and scarves.

Whatcha Do: Form two groups and have them stand facing each other. Place identical junk piles between the lines. Choose someone to be the caller. The caller will call out the name of an item in the junk pile and give an instruction such as "Hat—put it on!" or "Pillow—bop the person next to you!" The first player in each line finds the item and follows the direction, then passes the item to the next player in line, who also follows the directions. The last person in line places the item back in the junk pile and then the caller begins again with another item. Play until each piece of junk from the junk piles has been used at least one time. Then choose a new caller and form new lines.

ON YOUR TIPTOES!
Even older children like this simple game.

Whatcha Need: You'll need paper plates or sheets of paper.

Whatcha Do: Have children remove their shoes (and even their socks if they'd like). Hand each child a paper plate to place on the floor. Be sure the plates are scattered apart. Explain that the object of this game is to get everyone's toes on a paper plate. When you call "Go toes!" all children rush to put their toes on a paper plate. After the first call, remove a paper plate and play again. Children must move away from the plates before returning! Continue calling and removing paper plates until only one plate remains. Call again and the person with her toes on the plate first gets to choose the next game. For a fun twist, play with fingers or even elbows touching the plates!

 # SKYBALL
Older kids love this high-energy outdoor game.

Whatcha Need: You'll need a playground ball and two jump ropes.

Whatcha Do: Place the jump ropes at opposite ends of the playing area at least 30 feet apart. Have children count off by fours to make a Ones team, Twos team, Threes team, and Fours team. Have all the players stand in the center and hand the ball to someone. The ball is tossed as high to the sky as possible. When it's caught, the player catching it tries to run across either jump-rope line to score a point for his team. Members of the other teams try to intercept the ball or to knock it from the runner's hands. The runner may pass the ball to someone else, who then becomes the chasee. The first team to score 6 points wins and may choose the next game.

 # STEPPING-STONES
This simple relay is ideal for very young children.

Whatcha Need: You'll need paper plates.

Whatcha Do: Have children form pairs and stand at one end of the room or play area. Hand each pair four paper-plate stepping-stones. Explain that the object of this relay is to get to the opposite end of the room by stepping on pretend stepping-stones instead of the floor. Demonstrate how to set down a stepping-stone, step on it, lay down another stone, step on it, and so on. Encourage partners to help each other keep their balance and set down their stones. When everyone has made it across the room and back, try this variation. Have each set of partners use only two stepping-stones and see if they can make it across the room and back. What cooperative fun!

GOODIES GALORE

Lip-smacking s'mores, flowerpot cupcakes, rainbow pinwheels, and "munch" more are recipes for classroom cooperation and tasty fun.

A Bit of Background

Add a classroom full of kids, a pound of learning, a dash of tasty food, and a bit of frolic and what do you have? A winning recipe for classroom fun! And it's the kind of delicious fun your kids can't wait to sink their teeth into. Kids and cooking go together like cookies and milk! Cooking experiences and snack preparation are a great alternative to classroom crafts and make any Sunday school program or VBS more exciting and motivating. And kids can learn a lot from the simplest of snack preparation, including

- following directions,
- teamwork,
- working toward a cooperative goal, and
- responsibility for cleanup.

Great goodies are as fun to make as they are to eat. Look for no-cook recipes and recipes that don't use sharp knives for the best results. Fruits and vegetables lend themselves perfectly for yogurt-based dips and spreads—and kids love the crunch! Cheeses and cold cuts look super when cut with cookie cutters and are fun to pile on crackers or flour tortillas. Use pretzel sticks instead of toothpicks to make crazy fruit kabobs or food sculptures.

Consider letting your kids make their own classroom recipe books to take home at the end of the year. Each time you prepare a snazzy snack, hand out recipe cards and let kids copy the recipe and directions, then draw a quick picture of the goodie. Punch holes in the upper left-hand corners of the cards and connect the cards with giant paper clips or slip them on key chains. Encourage kids to try their new snack ideas at home and share them with the family—but remind your young chefs to keep kitchens clean and sparkling after their cooking adventures!

Keep in mind these quick-n-easy cooking tips!

★ **Make aprons in a snap by cutting plastic garbage bags in half and taping them in place at the waist.**

★ **Try using the "assembly-line" technique. Designate small groups of kids to stand in line and assemble sandwiches by first placing bread on plates, then adding lettuce, then cheese, and so on. This technique works great!**

★ **Use plastic self-locking bags to mix dough, trail mix, juices, or other ingredients for recipes.**

★ **Keep damp sponges at hand for emergency drips and drops!**

PITA-POCKET ARKS

Whatcha Need: You'll need pita pockets, small animal-shaped cookie cutters, lettuce, and sliced luncheon meats.

Whatcha Do: Let children use the animal-shaped cookie cutters to cut small animal shapes from luncheon meats. Shred lettuce for hay and stuff it in the bottoms of the Pita-Pocket Arks. Place the edible animals on top. If you'd like, provide condiments such as ketchup, mustard, or mayonnaise. Add to the fun with another of these Pita-Pocket Ark ideas:

● Decorate the top edges of pita pockets with tube icing. Then place pairs of animal crackers inside the pita arks.

● Set out various snack foods as pretend animals. Include snacks such as raisins, fruit and vegetable slices, or crackers.

RED SEA SIPPERS

Whatcha Need: You'll need Ziploc sandwich bags, drinking straws, milk, and sweetened cherry soft drink mix.

Whatcha Do: Have children work in pairs. To make a Red Sea Sipper, hold open the Ziploc bag and pour in 1½ cups of milk, then sprinkle in 3 tablespoons of cherry soft drink mix. Seal the bag securely and shake it gently to mix the ingredients. Open the bag slightly at one end and slip in a straw to sip and enjoy. In the summer, add a scoop of vanilla ice cream and make the Red Sea really frothy!

Try using different flavors of soft drink mix such as wild berry, grape, tiki punch, or a daring combination of several flavors!

TRINITY S'MORES

Whatcha Need: You'll need refrigerator sugar-cookie dough, chocolate candy kisses, mini-marshmallows, cookie sheets, and an oven. Preheat the oven to 325 degrees.

Whatcha Do: Slice ½ inch of sugar cookie dough for each child. Have children flatten the dough to make 3-inch circles about ¼ inch thick. Unwrap the chocolate kisses and place one kiss and a mini-marshmallow in the center of each dough circle. Pull the edges of the cookie up so they cover the candy and marshmallow. Pinch the dough to seal the cookie. Point out how this is a three-in-one cookie just as the Trinity is three-in-one and one-in-three. Place cookies on a cookie sheet and bake for 12 minutes or until golden brown. As the cookies cool, remind children that the Trinity is made up of God the Father, Jesus, and the Holy Spirit. Just as the cookies are three-in-one (marshmallows, cookie dough, and candy kisses), the Trinity is three-in-one.

CONFETTI FRUITS

Whatcha Need: You'll need fresh chunks of apple and banana, canned pineapple chunks (drained), maraschino cherries, paper plates, party toothpicks, and several fruit flavors of powdered gelatin mix.

Whatcha Do: Pour the powdered gelatin onto the paper plates. Poke each fruit chunk with a party toothpick, then roll it in the powdered gelatin. Place the sparkly fruits on a paper plate or bright plastic plate and enjoy!

Try including other fruits such as mangoes, papayas, and even grapes—but be sure they're a bit damp when dipped.

 FLOWERPOT CUPCAKES

Whatcha Need: You'll need cake mix, plastic spoons, aluminum foil, canned icing, plastic forks, candy sprinkles, an oven, and one new 4-inch clay pot for each child. Prepare the cake mix beforehand so it's ready to spoon into the pots. Preheat the oven to 350 degrees.

Whatcha Do: For each cupcake, place a piece of foil inside the pot to cover the hole at the bottom. Spoon in cake batter until the pot is ¾ full. Bake the cupcake for 15 minutes or until the cake springs back when lightly touched. (Have an adult do this.) Cool for 15 minutes, then ice and decorate with candy sprinkles. Eat the cupcake from the pot with a plastic fork. Share your fun by trying one of these ideas:

● Decorate the flowerpots after the cupcakes have cooled, then present the goodies and packets of flower seeds to the church office staff.

● Use a larger pot to bake a cake for the church picnic.

 RAINBOW PINWHEELS

Whatcha Need: You'll need two packages of refrigerator sugar-cookie dough, food coloring, waxed paper, cookie sheets, granulated sugar, a sharp knife, and access to an oven and refrigerator. Preheat the oven to 375 degrees.

Whatcha Do: Divide each tube of dough into fourths. Knead red food coloring into two of the sections, then combine them to make a long narrow log. Knead yellow food coloring into two more sections and combine them. Then roll out the yellow dough and wrap it completely around the red log. Repeat the process for the next sections of dough, adding green-colored dough around the yellow layer and blue-colored dough around the green. Wrap the log with waxed paper and chill it for 30 minutes. Then slice the dough into ¼-inch-wide circles and place them on a cookie sheet. Bake about 7 minutes, watching carefully so the cookies don't turn brown. Remove cookies from the oven and sprinkle them with sugar. Cool and enjoy.

VEGGIE-TACO TRIANGLES

Whatcha Need: You'll need pita pockets, shredded lettuce and red cabbage, shredded cheese, chopped olives and tomatoes, shredded carrots, chopped red and green peppers, drained beets, plastic knives, and paper plates.

Whatcha Do: Cut each pita pocket in half to make triangle shapes. Set out the paper plates and bowls of the vegetables and cheese. Invite children to build a colorful veggie-taco triangle to munch. Encourage children to try at least one new food in their tacos. Older children may wish to help clean and cut the vegetables. Younger children can use plastic knives to cut the pitas in half.

STICKY STARS

Whatcha Need: You'll need marshmallow creme, hot water, Ziploc sandwich bags, and assorted dry cereals.

Whatcha Do: Heat the marshmallow creme by running the jar under hot water until it's smooth and a bit runny. Fill the plastic sandwich bags half full of dry cereal. Drizzle about ¼ cup of thinned marshmallow creme over the cereal, then tightly seal the plastic bags. Gently knead the cereal mixture back and forth to spread the marshmallow creme. As it spreads, the creme will become thicker and stickier. When the cereal starts to stick together, form a large star shape with the bagged cereal. Then open the bag and munch away!

Try adding bits of dried fruit to the mixture. Mmm good!

PAINTED TOASTY TREATS

Whatcha Need: You'll need milk, food coloring, new paintbrushes, paper cups, white bread, plastic knives, cinnamon sugar, margarine, and a toaster.

Whatcha Do: Place several drops of food coloring in each paper cup and add ¼ cup milk to each color. Use paintbrushes to paint simple designs on slices of bread. Try painting favorite Bible characters, Bible scenes, or Christian symbols such as the Ichthus, hearts, a cross, or a dove. Toast the bread lightly, then spread on margarine and sprinkle cinnamon sugar over the tasty toast.

MONKEY TAILS

Whatcha Need: You'll need fresh bananas, plastic knives, melted chocolate, chocolate candy sprinkles, new craft sticks, and waxed paper. You'll also need access to a freezer.

Whatcha Do: Peel the bananas and cut them in half. Poke a craft stick through each banana half from the flat side upward. Dip the bananas in the melted chocolate, then roll them in chocolate candy sprinkles. Place the monkey tails on waxed paper and freeze them at least 30 minutes before eating.

Try one of these cool variations for frozen bananas. They're sure winners for chilly summer fun!

● Dip fresh bananas in honey, then roll them in crushed peanuts or candy sprinkles before freezing.

● Make Abominable Snowmen by dipping bananas in honey, then rolling them in shredded coconut before freezing.

 # EDIBLE ROSE PETALS

Whatcha Need: You'll need fresh-picked rose petals (grown without garden spray), water, a plastic bag, waxed paper, granulated sugar, fresh blueberries, and shoestring licorice. You'll also need access to a freezer.

Whatcha Do: Gently rinse off the rose petals, but leave them damp. Pour a cup of granulated sugar in the plastic bag, put the rose petals in the bag, and shake the bag until the rose petals are coated with glittery sugar. Then place the petals on waxed paper and freeze for several minutes. While the rose petals chill, rinse and pat dry the blueberries.

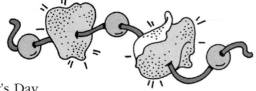

After several minutes, carefully string the blueberries and sparkly rose petals on the shoestring licorice for a colorful and unique snack. Be sure to remind children never to eat anything from outside without first checking with an adult.

These beautiful edible "necklaces" make lovely Mother's Day gifts—memorable and delicious!

 # CANDY CLAY

Whatcha Need: You'll need ⅓ cup margarine, ⅓ cup light corn syrup, ½ teaspoon salt, 1 teaspoon vanilla, a box of powdered sugar, waxed paper, food coloring, mixing bowls, and graham crackers.

Whatcha Do: Mix all the ingredients together with clean hands, then knead the mixture until it's smooth. If the dough is sticky, add more powdered sugar. To make different colors of clay, pull off lumps of clay and knead in food coloring. Then pinch off bits of clay to make animals, flowers, or other shapes and designs as decorations for the graham crackers. See if you can create a scene from your favorite Bible story! Keep leftover dough in an air-tight container or plastic bag. Candy clay will stay fresh for several days.

For another tasty variation of edible dough, mix 1 cup creamy peanut butter with 1 box of powdered sugar. Add powdered sugar if the dough is sticky or a bit of water or milk if the dough is too dry. Store the dough in a plastic bag—if there's any left!

DELICIOUS DIPS

Whatcha Need: You'll need bowls, spoons, pretzel sticks (instead of toothpicks), and fruits, vegetables, or crackers. You'll also need the ingredients listed with each dip.

Whatcha Do: Follow the simple directions for each fabulous dip.
- **Rooty-Tooty-Fruity Dip:** Mix together a container of fruit-flavored yogurt and a small box of fruit-flavored gelatin mix. Let the mixture sit several minutes, then skewer fruits on pretzel sticks, dip, and devour!
- **Garden Vegetable Dip:** Mix together a small container of sour cream, a small jar of mayonnaise, and one package of vegetable soup mix. Let sit for half an hour, then dip crunchy vegetables, crackers, or fresh bread in this tasty treat.

- **Dessert Dip:** Mix 1 cup of chocolate syrup and ½ cup of strawberry preserves. Dip fresh fruits or crackers in this amazing dip.

LOCUSTS & HONEY

Whatcha Need: You'll need refrigerator biscuit dough, melted butter, a pastry brush, honey, paper plates, raisins, cookie sheets, and access to an oven. Preheat the oven to 425 degrees.

Whatcha Do: Separate the dough into biscuits and shape the biscuits into pretend locusts or grasshoppers. Use raisins for eyes. Place the critters on cookie sheets and brush them with melted butter. Bake the dough for 10 minutes or until the biscuits are golden brown. Dip the pretend locusts in honey for a terrific taste treat that even John the Baptist would have gobbled up!

MANNA MUNCHIE SQUARES

Whatcha Need: You'll need graham crackers, marshmallow creme, almond flavoring, a cookie sheet, a mixing bowl, a spoon, waxed paper, sesame seeds, and a sharp knife. If you have a large group to feed, use several boxes of graham cracker-flavored cereal instead of graham crackers.

Whatcha Do: Soften the marshmallow creme by setting the jar in hot water for several minutes. Coarsely crumble several packages of graham crackers in a large mixing bowl. Add ½ cup sesame seeds to the graham crackers. Stir 3 teaspoons of almond flavoring into the jar of marshmallow creme. Drizzle the creme over the graham crackers and seeds, then mix thoroughly. Line a cookie sheet with waxed paper and spread the graham-cracker mixture on the lined cookie sheet. Chill at least 20 minutes or until the manna isn't too sticky. Cut into 3-inch squares and enjoy.

While kids nibble, read from Exodus 16 about how God fed his people manna. Remind everyone that this manna is yummy but that only God made real bread from heaven!

FIGS IN A BLANKET

Whatcha Need: You'll need clean lettuce leaves, dried figs (pitted), softened cream cheese, party toothpicks, and plastic knives.

Whatcha Do: Gently slice a dried fig lengthwise, being careful not to cut through the fig. Stuff the dried fig with softened cream cheese, then roll the plump fig in a lettuce leaf and secure it with a party toothpick. Make plenty, then share this wholesome biblical treat with another class as you read the story about Jesus and a fig tree from Matthew 21:18-22.

Try stuffing pitted dates, pitted prunes, and dried apricots with softened cream cheese or cottage cheese. Wrap the goodies in fresh lettuce leaves, grape leaves, or cabbage leaves.

SUNNY SMILES

Whatcha Need: You'll need rice cakes, peanut butter, chocolate chips, raisins, mini-marshmallows, plastic knives, paper plates, and thin apple slices cut from apple wedges.

Whatcha Do: For each smiling face, spread peanut butter on a rice cake. Add raisins and chocolate chips for eyes and noses. Place a sliced apple wedge on for a smiling mouth, then spread a bit of peanut butter on the apple wedge and add mini-marshmallows for a toothy grin. Serve each other Sunny Smiles on paper plates—with a smile!

Other rice-cake goodies that'll make you smile:
● Mix softened cream cheese with strawberry preserves and spread this sweet treat on rice cakes.
● Spread a thin layer of cheddar cheese spread on a rice cake and pile on the raw veggies! Yummy and oh so healthy!

MINI LOLLI-BOUQUETS

Whatcha Need: You'll need a bag of store-bought sugar cookies or vanilla wafer cookies, canned icing, plastic knives, ribbon, new craft sticks, and candy decorations such as tiny red-hots, gumdrops, candy corn, mini-M&M's, or raisins. Snip candies with clean scissors to make colorful, tiny snippets.

Whatcha Do: For each lolli, spread icing on the backs of two cookies and sandwich a craft stick between them. Decorate the lollis with candy bits, using icing as glue. Prepare three lollis, then tie them together with colorful ribbon.

Try using ice cream or a mixture of cream cheese and canned icing as the filling between cookies. Chill the cookie sandwiches, then devour them!

SALAD GLOVES

Whatcha Need: You'll need new pairs of solid-colored, cotton garden gloves, permanent markers, several bowls of salad dressing, and a variety of salad bar foods, including sunflower seeds, shredded or chopped carrots, lettuce, celery, garbanzo beans, croutons, green pepper rings, olives, and cheese cubes. You'll need one new pair of garden gloves for each child.

Whatcha Do: Give each child a pair of garden gloves. Use permanent markers to decorate the garden gloves with designs of your favorite vegetables or other healthy foods. For example, show a carrot along one finger of the glove, cauliflower on the palm, and a cherry tomato on the thumb. Then set out the salad bar items and have each child assemble a mini-salad on one gloved hand. Dip vegetables in salad dressing for extra flavor and fun. When you are through nibbling your salad bar goodies, wear your new gloves to plant a vegetable or flower garden!

SOUP-SHARE 20

Whatcha Need: You'll need a large cooking pot, several cans of beef or chicken broth, spoons, Styrofoam cups, barley or rice, salt and pepper, water, a can of chopped tomatoes, dried parsley, crackers, and chopped raw vegetables such as carrots, celery, potatoes, and cabbage. You'll also need access to a hot plate, electric skillet, or stove.

Whatcha Do: Place the broth and tomatoes in a large cooking pot. Add 2 cups of water, 1 cup of barley or rice, and the raw vegetables you've chosen. Be sure the vegetables are cut into bite-sized pieces. Add ¼ cup dried parsley and salt and pepper to taste. Bring the soup to a boil, then cover and simmer for 1 hour or more, stirring occasionally. Share your soup with lots of friends by serving it in colorful Styrofoam cups with lots of crackers. Have kids tell one thing they've shared with someone else, then something they're glad God has shared with us.

CINNAMON HEARTS 21

Whatcha Need: You'll need two cans of applesauce, a large mixing bowl, waxed paper, spoons, three envelopes of Knox gelatin, heart-shaped cookie cutters, a cookie sheet, hot water, and cinnamon.

Whatcha Do: Prepare the Knox gelatin in a mixing bowl, using half the hot water called for in the directions. Stir in 2 cans of applesauce and 3 tablespoons of cinnamon. Line a cookie sheet with waxed paper. Spread the applesauce mixture on the cookie sheet. Chill for 1 hour, then peel the rubbery gelatin from the waxed paper. Use heart shaped-cookie cutters to cut out yummy spicy hearts. Mmm good!

FUNNY BUNNIES

Whatcha Need: You'll need large marshmallows, toothpicks, clean scissors, lettuce leaves or cupcakes, and red food coloring.

Whatcha Do: Using clean scissors, make a short diagonal cut in the upper right corner of a large marshmallow. (See figure 1.) Be careful not to cut clear through the marshmallow! Carefully lift the corner of the marshmallow and snip down the center to make rabbit ears. (See figure 2.) Gently spread the ears apart. From the place you made your first snip, make another snip going straight down to the middle of the marshmallow. This will form the tail, so pinch it a bit to make it round and fluffy. (See figure 3.) Make a short snip halfway between the base of the ears and the bottom of the marshmallow to make the bunny's face. (See figure 4.) Make a diagonal snip in the lower left corner of the marshmallow to make the bunny's legs. (See figure 5.) Finally, use a toothpick dipped in red food coloring to make eyes, a nose, and bunny whiskers. Set your bunnies on lettuce leaves or on top of cupcakes for cute Easter decorations.

PIES IN A POUCH

Whatcha Need: You'll need Ziploc bags, whipped cream, cinnamon, canned pumpkin, graham crackers, and plastic spoons.

Whatcha Do: Crumble several packages of graham crackers. For each pie, open a Ziploc bag and measure in ¼ cup canned pumpkin, ½ cup whipped cream, and ⅛ teaspoon cinnamon. Seal the bag securely, then gently mix the ingredients by kneading them back and forth. Open the bag and add ¼ cup graham cracker crumbles. Eat the pies in a pouch with plastic spoons.

    For more exciting flavors, try one of these pleasin' pie ideas:

    ● Add ½ cup each of fruit yogurt and whipped cream. Mix in fresh bananas or strawberry preserves. Crumble graham crackers on top, then enjoy.

    ● Add ½ cup cherry or blueberry pie filling and ½ cup whipped cream into a Ziploc bag. Mix and then add ¼ cup graham cracker crumbles. Deee-licious!

CANDY CANE COOKIES

Whatcha Need: You'll need two tubes of refrigerator sugar-cookie dough, red food coloring, crushed candy canes, a knife, cookie sheets, and access to an oven. Preheat the oven to 350 degrees.

Whatcha Do: For each cookie, slice off two 1-inch lumps of cookie dough. Knead red food coloring into one of the lumps. Roll each lump of dough into a 6-inch-long and ½-inch-thick rope. Pinch the ropes together at one end, then twist the red and white dough as if making a curved candy cane. Place the cookies on a cookie sheet, then gently push a sprinkling of crushed candy cane into the dough. Bake about 8 minutes, being careful that the cookies don't turn brown. Remove the cookies from the oven and allow them to cool before eating.

For a festive service project, bake more candy cane cookies, place them in plastic bags, and tie the bags shut with red and white curled ribbons. Present the cookies to special friends or community helpers.

BANANA BOATS 25

Whatcha Need: You'll need aluminum foil, cookie sheets, bananas, small marshmallows, chocolate chips, shredded coconut, and plastic spoons. You'll also need access to an oven or an outdoor grill.

Whatcha Do: These warm snacks make cool autumn cookouts special. For each Banana Boat, peel back a narrow strip of the banana peel, being careful to keep the peel attached to the banana. Scoop out several spoonfuls of banana and fill the groove with small marshmallows and chocolate chips. Sprinkle the marshmallows and chocolate chips with shredded coconut. Fold the banana peel back over the goodies. Then carefully wrap the banana in aluminum foil.

If you're using an oven, place the foil-wrapped bananas on cookie sheets and bake the Banana Boats at 300 degrees for 15 minutes. If you're using an outdoor grill, place the foil-wrapped Banana Boats direcly on the metal grate and heat for 15 minutes.

After heating the Banana Boats, let them cool for several minutes. Then remove the foil, peel back the banana flap, and enjoy!

PRAYER & WORSHIP

Creative prayers and worship activities to encourage kids to deepen their faith as they draw nearer to God!

A Bit of Background

Prayer and worship are natural and necessary parts of any children's Christian education program. But though essential, they're not always easy to teach in creative ways. Some think that prayer is an inborn ability not requiring formal or creative instruction. But just as Jesus taught his followers how to pray in Luke 11:1, children need prayer instruction too. Inspire prayer confidence in kids by assuring them it's fine to sit, kneel, or stand while praying and that it's equally fine to pray silently or aloud. Point out that people have different ways of speaking to God through prayer and that what matters most is not the method in which they pray, but the sincerity of their prayers.

Help kids learn to pray for a group by pairing children and having them thank God aloud for their partners. The next time you meet, increase the pairs to trios and so on until the group is gathered as one. Ask for volunteers to pray aloud for the entire group and thank God for the time you have to share with each other. Soon, your kids will be clamoring for a turn to pray for the group! Never force a shy child to pray aloud—remember, prayer is a personal expression and not everyone is comfortable praying aloud.

Here are some biblical "prayer reminders" to pass along to your kids:

● God hears our prayers. (Proverbs 15:29b)
● God answers our prayers. (Mark 11:24)
● We're to pray for others. (Colossians 1:9)
● We pray in Jesus' name. (John 14:13)
● We're to pray faithfully. (1 Thessalonians 5:17)

Worship can be a confusing and often boring part of church for many children. It's not that kids and worship don't go together but that kids may have a difficult time understanding why they're worshiping. Stress that we worship God for who he is and for what he does. By discovering what God does, children better understand who God is—and vice versa! Begin the year by listing all the things God does and can do, such as healing, helping, protecting, providing, loving, and forgiving. Then help children turn those actions into names for God, such as "God, our helper" or "our loving God." Encourage children to address God in these ways during worship and even in their prayers. By helping children understand what God does and who he is, we're drawing them closer to God in heart, mind, and spirit.

Prayer and worship are two of the most joy-filled ways we express our love to and for our loving Father. Have fun helping your children build a prayerful, powerful, worshipful lifestyle that will draw them ever nearer to God!

WELCOME BELLS

Welcoming others to worship
Psalm 100:4

Whatcha Need: You'll need a Bible, newspapers, bowls of water, paper towels, acrylic paints, small paintbrushes or toothpicks, and small brass bells (available at craft stores). You'll need one bell for each child.

Whatcha Know!

Jingle and jangle your call-to-worship bells as you chant the worship chant (#2). Ask the minister if your group can present their musical greeting at the start of the worship service. Store the bells under the pews afterward.

Whatcha Do: Cover a table with newspaper and set out the water, the acrylic paints, and the paintbrushes or toothpicks. Tell children that one Christian custom many churches observe is a call to worship. Point out that many churches have steeples with bells or chimes that ring when it's time to begin worship services. Explain that bells and chimes have a sweet welcoming sound and signal Christians that it's time to praise and honor God together. Read aloud Psalm 100:4, then invite children to paint the brass bells with pretty designs. When children want to change colors of paint, have them daub their paintbrushes on paper towels after rinsing them. Set the bells aside until the next worship time, then invite children to come to church several minutes early and greet people with a call to worship. Line the entryway with your special bell-ringers and have children verbally greet people with "Welcome to worship," "Glad you're here," and "God loves you!"

THE WORSHIP CHANT

Reasons we worship God
John 4:24

Whatcha Need: You'll need a Bible, poster board, markers, and a pair of white gloves for each child. Use white cotton garden gloves or purchase stretchy one-size-fits-all gloves from discount stores.

Whatcha Do: Before class, write the words to the Worship Chant that follows on a large sheet of poster board. To begin, visit about the reasons we worship God. Remind children that we worship God for who he is and for what he does. Tell children that we worship God in spirit and in truth, then read aloud John 4:24. Give each child a pair of gloves, then lead children in the accompanying hand motions as they repeat the Worship Chant. After children are familiar with the words and motions, offer to present the Worship Chant to the entire congregation to remind them why we worship God.

Worship Chant

Group 1: We worship God for who he is. *(Point upward and wave fingers in the air.)*
Group 2: Hosanna, praise the Lord! *(Put hands over hearts, point to lips, then raise hands in the air and clap two times.)*

Group 1: We worship God for what he does. *(Repeat motions.)*
Group 2: All in one accord! *(Repeat motions.)*
Group 1: His name we praise, *(Cup hands around mouths.)*
Group 2: His glory raise. *(Point upward.)*
Unison: We'll worship God through all our days! *(Clap and turn around.)*
Group 1: We worship God to show our love. *(Point upward and wave fingers in the air.)*
Group 2: Hosanna, praise the Lord! *(Put hands over hearts, point to lips, then raise hands in the air and clap two times.)*

TRINITY TRIANGLES
We worship God, Jesus, and the Holy Spirit.
Matthew 28:19

Whatcha Need: You'll need a Bible, an old book of wallpaper samples, poster board or cardboard, scissors, glue, fishing line, tape, and plastic drinking straws. Cut out a large poster-board triangle.

Whatcha Do: Set the triangle beside you and ask children what things come in sets of three. Suggestions might include tricycle wheels, silverware settings, the Three Little Pigs or The Three Musketeers, triplets, and triangles. Hold up the paper triangle and explain that God is in three persons: God the Father, Jesus his Son, and the Holy Spirit. Explain that this is the Trinity or Godhead. Read aloud Matthew 28:19. Then ask children what each member of the Trinity does for us. Point to each side of the triangle as you remind children that God is our creator and all-powerful Father. Jesus is God's Son who died for our sins so we could be forgiven and live with God in heaven. And the Holy Spirit was sent to us after Jesus died to help us do the things Jesus would do if he were still on earth. Explain that when we worship God, we're worshiping the Trinity too.

Invite children to make Trinity triangle mobiles to remind them of the Trinity and that when we worship God we worship all the members of the Trinity at once. Glue wallpaper to the front and back of poster board, then cut triangles out of the poster board. Tape fishing line between the triangles or cut slots in the shapes and connect them for a three-dimensional look. Suspend the triangles from drinking straws, then hang the mobiles from the ceiling in the worship area.

CIRCLE OF PRAYER
Prayer draws us near to God.
Matthew 18:20

Whatcha Need: You'll need a Bible.

Whatcha Do: Gather children in a circle and ask why we pray. Remind children that prayer is a way to worship God and talk to him. Explain that when we pray, we draw near to God and know that he's near to us. Read aloud Matthew 18:20, then point out that when we gather together in the Lord's name, he promises to be with us. Place the Bible on a chair in the center of the room and have children stand in a circle around the chair. Tell children that you'll offer a prayer of thanksgiving to God and that each time they hear the words "near" or "close," they are to take a step toward the Bible. Pray: **Dear God, we thank you for the gift of prayer. We know that prayer draws us *near* to you. We thank you for times we can pray together, for we know that together prayers bring us even more *close* to you and to each other. Thank you, God, for staying *near* to us and for loving us.** Have children join hands and gently give their neighbors' hands a squeeze as you all say, "amen."

A PRAYERFUL PLACE

Places to pray
Mark 1:35

Whatcha Need: You'll need a Bible, scraps of felt, ruffles or lace, Tacky craft glue, and one carpet square for each child. Most carpet retailers are happy to give away free sample squares of their discontinued carpet styles. Pick low-nap carpets—and pick up plenty!

Whatcha Do: Ask children to tell about their favorite places to pray, such as cuddled in bed, in church, or in a quiet corner of their bedrooms. Ask children if they know where Jesus might have prayed, then read aloud Mark 1:35; Matthew 14:22, 23; 26:36; and Luke 6:12. Ask children why they think Jesus wanted to have quiet time with God. Then explain that God likes it when we pray with others, but God also thinks it's very special when we come to him alone with our prayers. Point out that Jesus had quiet prayerful places to pray. Then invite children to make their own prayerful places by gluing colorful felt shapes to the carpet squares. If you'd like, glue ruffles or lace around the edges.

Explain to children that these special carpet squares will help them remember to find quiet prayerful places to be alone with God, just as Jesus was alone with God. When the squares are finished, have children find places in the room to sit on their squares and pray.

THE RINGS OF PRAYER

Praying for others
Colossians 1:9

Whatcha Need: You'll need a Bible, four plastic finger-rings for each child, white poster paint, paintbrushes, and colorful fine-tipped markers. Look in a discount store's party department for inexpensive plastic rings with flat tops. Paint the flat tops white and allow them to dry thoroughly.

Whatcha Do: Ask children to name some of the people they've prayed for. Tell children that we can pray for ourselves, but God also wants us to pray for our families, for other people in the world, and even for people we might not get along with. Read aloud Colossians 1:9, then ask:

● **Why do you think God wants us to pray for others?**

● **How does praying for others draw us nearer to God? to others?**

Hand each child four plastic flat-topped rings. Explain that you'll be making prayer rings as reminders of who we can pray for. On the first ring, have children use fine-tipped markers to draw tiny pictures of themselves. On the next ring, have children draw tiny pictures of their families or someone in their families. On the third ring, have children draw a tiny picture of the world. And on the last ring, have children draw a red heart to symbolize God's love and help. Tell children to place the rings on their fingers and then say a silent prayer for each person or group of people the rings represent. For example, for the world rings, children might pray for someone in their school or community, for peace in a war-torn land, or for hungry children in the world. Remind children to end their prayers by expressing love and thanks to God. Challenge children to wear their rings for several days to remind them of the many people God calls us to pray for.

FEAST OF BLESSINGS

Worshiping with thanksgiving
Psalm 69:30

Whatcha Need: You'll need a Bible, large boxes or blankets, crackers, and slices of fruit.

Whatcha Do: Tell children that today you'll explore how God's people long ago worshiped God. Explain that people in Old Testament times gathered for special feasts to worship God for all the blessings he gave them. Then read aloud Psalm 69:30 and Leviticus 23:40-43. Ask children to name some of the blessings the Israelites might have worshiped God for. Then have children form small groups and make shelters from boxes or blankets. If you wish, decorate the boxes with markers and scraps of construction paper. Have children sit in their shelters and discuss the following questions:

● **How are God's blessings different today? the same?**

● **How did the people worship and honor God back then?**

● **What are ways we worship and honor God today?**

Share a prayer thanking God for his blessings in your lives. Then enjoy a feast as children munch crackers and fruit slices. Ask children how this feast is like and unlike Communion services at your church. Point out that gathering in the Lord's name for feasts, Communion, prayers, or just fun together-times draws us closer to God and are ways to worship him.

> ## Whatcha Know!
>
> This is a super summertime activity! Set up tents and hold a half-day Feast of Blessings as kids pray, play, and share great food.

EXPRESS YOURSELF!

Being still before God
Psalm 46:10

Whatcha Need: You'll need a Bible, markers, white paper, and a 12-inch clear vinyl square for each child. Purchase clear vinyl by the yard at craft or fabric stores. You'll also want quiet instrumental music playing in the background.

Whatcha Do: Have children find quiet places in the room. Softly tell children that worship isn't just something we do—it's also a way we feel inside when we approach God. Read Psalm 46:10. Ask children why it's hard to listen or concentrate when we're noisy or busy or bustling about our day. Invite children to spend quiet time thinking about God. Hand out the squares of clear vinyl, sheets of paper, and markers. Place the white paper under the vinyl squares and invite children to draw pictures on the vinyl that express how they feel toward God's love and power. As they contemplate and draw, play soft music in the background.

Allow at least 10 minutes to draw, then invite children to hold up their drawings and tell one word to describe God, such as powerful, loving, and creator. Arrange the vinyl squares on a large window. They will cling to the glass without tape and make a wonderful, worshipful expression of the children's quiet time with God.

WORSHIP WORDS

Worshiping in our church
1 Chronicles 16:29

Whatcha Need: You'll need a Bible, newsprint, white paper, scissors, markers, and worship items your church typically uses.

Whatcha Do: Bring in items your church uses during worship services. Items might include a collection plate, utensils for Communion, a special Bible, candles, an incense censor, an ephod, or other articles of clothing. Invite your minister to visit with children about these items and their significance for worship in your church. Encourage children to ask questions. As each item is described, write its name on a sheet of newsprint and invite children to repeat its name.

When all the worship items have been shown, demonstrate how to fold and cut a book from a sheet of white paper, then help kids create their own books. You may wish to enlist the help of several adult volunteers for the folding and cutting. Explain that these paper books will be dictionaries to remind children of the items in your church's worship services. Have children write the name of one item on each page, then draw a picture of that item. Older children can put the words in their dictionaries in alphabetical order.

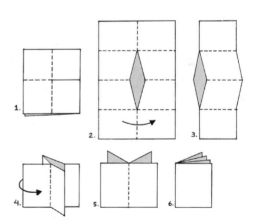

When the dictionaries are finished, take turns asking about certain items, challenging children to spell the words and to match the items with their worship significance. Encourage children to keep their special worship dictionaries in their Bibles for quick reference. Close by reading 1 Chronicles 16:29 and thanking God for providing your church as a place of worship.

KNIT TOGETHER IN PRAYER

Prayer knits us together.
1 Thessalonians 1:2

Whatcha Need: You'll need a Bible and a ball of yarn.

Whatcha Do: Invite children to stand in a circle. Hold up the yarn and ask what it is used for. Then ask:

● **In what ways does prayer knit us together like yarn knits a warm sweater?**

● **How can prayer bring people closer?**

● **What are things people pray for together?**

Read aloud 1 Thessalonians 1:2. Then have children each think of a sentence they could say as a prayer for the entire class. Suggest sentences such as "God, please help our faith grow" or "Lord, thank you for bringing us here to worship you." Say your own sentence to begin the group prayer, then hold the end of the yarn as you toss the ball of yarn to someone across the circle. Have that person add his prayer sentence and then hold onto the yarn and toss the ball of yarn to someone else. Continue knitting everyone together in prayer until everyone is holding a portion of the yarn.

End by having the last person with the ball of yarn say "amen," then tossing the ball in reverse order around the circle so everyone can say "amen" and wind up her portion of yarn.

Whatcha Know!

Invite children to use several balls of yarn and present this prayer activity to the adult congregation for the closing prayer in their worship service. Have children remind everyone that prayer knits us together in love and in the name of the Lord.

IN HIS TIME

God answers prayers.
Psalm 91:14, 15

Whatcha Need: You'll need a Bible, markers, and a small calendar for each child. Calendars are free at many insurance companies or you can make them on a computer. You'll also need several timepieces such as a stopwatch, an egg timer, and a clock with a second hand.

Whatcha Do: Place the timepieces so children can see them. Ask what each timepiece is used for, then tell children you'll give directions for doing certain things in a given time. Have children try to do the following in the indicated time frames.

● Tiptoe around the room three times in 1 minute.

● Tell three people that God loves them in 15 seconds.

● Shake the hands of everyone in class in 2 minutes.

● Tell one person about Jesus in the next week.

Gather children and explain that we can do most things in the time we plan. We can wash our hands in several minutes, practice the piano for an hour, or learn a Bible verse in a week. Ask children if they know how long it takes God to answer our prayers. Then read aloud Psalm 91:14, 15. Tell children that God always answers our prayers, but he answers them in his way and in his time.

That means that God chooses when he will answer each prayer—and it may not always be in the time frame we'd like.

Hand out the calendars and invite children to decorate them with markers. Challenge children to use the calendars to keep track of their prayers and when God answers them. Also remind children to thank God when he answers their prayers!

FAMILY WORSHIP LINKS
Families can worship God together.
Psalm 95:6

Whatcha Need: You'll need a Bible, ¼- and ½-inch plastic jewels, several bags of large paper clips, and Tacky craft glue.

Whatcha Do: Gather children and ask them to tell about the great things their families do together, such as going on picnics, attending church, sharing special meals, and hosting holiday celebrations. Then explain that one of the best things families can do together is pray and worship God. Read aloud Psalm 95:6. Then ask:

- **How does worshiping God join family members closer together? to God?**
- **In what ways can families worship God at home?**

Tell children that families worship God at home in many ways, such as helping each other, speaking kind words, praying, and reading the Bible. Hand each child thirty-one large paper clips. Demonstrate how to glue a plastic jewel on one end of a clip, then have children glue jewels to their paper clips. (If your class is large, use giant sequins instead.) As you work, explain that when these beautiful clips are joined together, they will form a family worship chain.

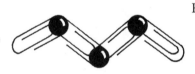

Point out that just as the clips are linked together, prayer and worship link families closer to God and to each other. Encourage children to add one link each time the family prays together, helps one another, is kind, or worships God in some way. Challenge children to see if they can add one link a day for an entire month.

STRONG FAITH!
Worship strengthens our faith.
Acts 4:24

Whatcha Need: You'll need a Bible.

Whatcha Do: Gather children and choose someone to sit on a chair in the center of the room. Ask if anyone thinks he can push the child and the chair across the room with one finger. Begin by trying to push the child and chair with one of your fingers, then ask another child to help. Keep adding children until, as a group, you're able to push the child in the chair across the room and back. Place the Bible in the chair, then ask:

- **Why were we able to finally push the chair?**
- **How does having many people help strengthen the group?**

● **How is this activity like people praying and worshiping together?**

Read aloud Acts 4:24. Explain that when many people gather in God's name to pray and worship, it strengthens everyone's faith. If there's time, read from Acts 12:1-11 how the early Christians prayed as a group for Peter's safety when he was in prison. Then invite children to gather in a group around the Bible and ask for volunteers to offer a prayer thanking God for the body of believers and how we can strengthen each other's faith through worship and prayer.

Whatcha Know!

Put your corporate strength together to do a big chore around the church, such as the spring cleaning, yard work, or helping move and rearrange the furniture in a room.

THE SPELLING SONG
Worship is joyful.
Psalm 100:2

Whatcha Need: You'll need a Bible, markers, and newsprint. Write the words to "The Spelling Song" on newsprint. Write the first letter in each line in red, and position the letters so that they read downward to spell out the word "worship."

Whatcha Do: Gather children and ask them how it feels to worship God. Explain that we can worship God with our words, our actions, and even our feelings. Point out that sometimes worship is a quiet time with God, but worship can also be a joyous, lively time with God. Read aloud Psalm 100:2, then invite children to chant, rap, or sing "The Spelling Song" to learn how to spell the word "worship" and also to express their joy in worshiping God in a lively way. Chant or rap the song through several times, then ask for volunteers to spell the word "worship" without reading from the newsprint. Everyone will be able to spell this important word—and feel the lively joy it brings—in no time at all!

Wave your hands
On the ground.
Raise your arms and turn around.
Smile and
Hop
Into the air—
Praise and love God everywhere!

CAN-DO PRAYERS

God can do anything.
Genesis 18:14

Whatcha Need: You'll need a Bible; clean, empty cans (without the labels); construction paper; white paper; tape; and markers. Be sure there are no rough edges around the tops of the cans. Cover the edges with duct tape if you desire.

Whatcha Do: Have children stand in a circle and hand each child an empty can. Give the following directions and challenge children to try to perform each action:
- Rub your tummy and pat your tin can at the same time.
- Say "toy boat" three times as you tap your can.
- Hop up and down and whistle a tune into your can.
- Hold your can behind you and give your elbow a kiss.

Have children sit down, then ask which direction was impossibly hard. Remind children that we can't do everything, but there is someone who can. Read aloud Genesis 18:14a, then explain that God can do anything because he is God. God's power is awesome, and he can do anything—even when we can't. Ask children to tell about times they were afraid or worried about something they couldn't do or had no control over. Point out that when we feel as if we can't, we know that God can if we trust him.

Invite children to cover the cans with construction paper, then write the words "God Can!" on the containers. As you work, explain that these are "Can-Do" cans to remind everyone that God can do anything. Hand out slips of paper and have children each write down one thing they're worried about or want to trust God to take care of. Place the papers in the Can-Do cans, then have children quietly pray about their particular needs. Remind children to trust God's power whenever they face things they can't do alone. End by challenging children to write down and pray about their "I can'ts" every day, then to put the papers in their "God Can!" containers as they trust God to do what they can't.

WAYS TO PRAISE

Praising God
Psalm 150

Whatcha Need: You'll need a Bible and items such as construction paper, markers, glue or tape, ribbons, and scissors.

Whatcha Do: Gather children and read aloud Psalm 150. Then ask what we can do to praise and honor God and to express our love for him. Suggest ways such as praying, singing, expressing our feelings through art, or even writing poems (or psalms) to God. Have children form small groups and brainstorm their own ways of honoring God. Invite the groups to use craft materials and paper to help. Allow several minutes for children to work, then have groups share their ways to praise. End by reminding children that worship and praise are as different and unique as the people who love God—and that God enjoys all ways to praise him!

God is powerful!

LIGHT THE WORLD
Prayer makes a difference.
2 Corinthians 5:20

Whatcha Need: You'll need a Bible, paper plates, markers, straight pins, clear tape, a newspaper or world news magazine, and one flashlight for each child. Have children bring their own flashlights or purchase inexpensive flashlights from a surplus store.

Whatcha Do: Set out the craft items and hand each child a flashlight. Tell children you'd like to "shed a little light" on some world issues, then invite children to help. When you read something positive from the newspaper or a world magazine, have children flash and wave their flashlights. When you read something sad or negative, have children turn off their lights. After several readings, set aside the flashlights. Then ask children how prayer can help the world and the people in other countries. Have children explain how God's love, through our prayers, can bring light to world darkness. Read aloud 2 Corinthians 5:20, then tell children that God wants us to pray for the world and for people who need to know and love Jesus. Ask children what other things we can pray for to bring God's light to the world and its people. Suggestions might include praying for others to know Jesus, for hunger to stop, and for peace for a war-torn country.

Hand each child two paper plates. Use the straight pins to poke holes in the plates and the markers to decorate the backs of the plates. Tape the front edges of the plates together but leave a small opening at the bottom. Slide the tip of each flashlight into the opening, then tape the flashlights to the paper plates. Darken the room and turn on the flashlights as you offer a prayer asking God to bring the light of his love to the world.

> ## Whatcha Know!
>
> Let young children hold these special love-lights at a Christmas Eve celebration instead of burning candles.

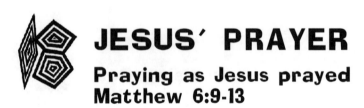

JESUS' PRAYER
Praying as Jesus prayed
Matthew 6:9-13

Whatcha Need: You'll need a Bible, five medium-sized boxes, white shelf paper, scissors, tape, and markers.

Whatcha Do: Ask children what's the best way to learn something. Lead children to suggest that showing or demonstrating how to do something is the best way to learn. Tell children that Jesus wanted us to learn how to pray, so he showed us how. Ask for a volunteer to read aloud Matthew 6:9-13. Then ask:
- **Why do you think Jesus taught us to pray?**
- **Why is it good to model our prayers after the way Jesus prayed?**

Explain that Jesus' prayer is almost like a love letter to God. His prayer begins with a greeting ("Our Father in heaven, hallowed be your name, your kingdom come, your will be done on earth as it is in heaven."). Next Jesus gives the body of the prayer, which includes needs and repentance ("Give us this day our daily bread. Forgive us our debts, as we also have forgiven our debtors."). Jesus also prays for God's strength ("And lead us not into temptation, but deliver us from the evil one."). Tell children that we often say a closing to God as well (For yours is the kingdom and the power and the glory forever. Amen.).

Have children form five groups. Hand each group a box. Direct children to cover their boxes with white paper, then have one group write the word "Greeting" on its box, another group write the word "Needs," another group the word "Forgiveness," another group the word "Strength," and the last group the word "Closing." Have group members copy on the boxes the corresponding words from the Lord's Prayer in Matthew 6:9-13, then decorate the boxes. Stack the boxes in order as a volunteer reads aloud Matthew 6:9-13. Keep the boxes stacked for the next several weeks to guide children in saying their own prayers to God.

PRAY EACH DAY
Pray regularly.
1 Thessalonians 5:17

Whatcha Need: You'll need a Bible.

Whatcha Do: Gather children and ask them how many times a day they perform various actions such as brushing their teeth, eating meals, or washing their hands. Then ask children why we do some things more than once a day. Point out that the Bible tells us how often we're to pray, then have a volunteer read aloud 1 Thessalonians 5:17. Encourage children to give reasons why they think God wants us to pray so often. Then teach children the words to this song. Sing it to the tune of "Jesus Loves Me."

Have children silently think of one thing they can pray about continually for the next week. Remind children that God hears our prayers but that he chooses the time and the way to answer them. Challenge children to keep praying their prayers until God chooses to answer.

We're to pray continually,
Not one time or two or three.
God will answer, wait and see—
If we're praying faithfully.
Pray every day,
Pray every day,
Pray every day,
God tells us that's the way.

20 WORSHIP RIBBONS
Worship is a lifestyle.
Psalm 96:9

Whatcha Need: You'll need a Bible, scissors, safety pins, small rubber bands, and ½-inch-wide ribbon in red, white, and purple.

Whatcha Do: Ask children to name the most important thing they can do to stay alive. Suggestions might include eating, drinking water, breathing, or resting. Tell children that just as these things are important to our physical life, worship is important to our life with God. We don't just breathe once or twice a week to stay alive—we must breathe all the time. Explain that we don't just worship God by attending church once or twice a week—we worship God every day by the things we do and say. Read aloud Psalm 96:9, then invite children to make special Worship Ribbon reminders to keep their worship of God alive and active.

For each ribbon, cut a 10-inch length of red, white, and purple ribbon. Use a rubber band to fasten the lengths of ribbon together at one end. Cut another 10-inch piece of ribbon and tie it in a bow around the rubber band. Point out that the white ribbon reminds us of God's pure power, the purple ribbon of Jesus' royalty, and the red ribbon of the fire of the Holy Spirit. Fasten a safety pin in back of the bow to pin to shirts, dresses, or jackets. If you prefer, use these ribbons as Bible bookmarks.

Whatcha Know!

For a neat church project, have your children prepare Worship Ribbons for other Sunday school classes or for the adult congregation to wear home!

DEVOTIONS & OBJECT LESSONS

Bible-bound lessons presented in snappy devotions and object lessons to keep kids growing and going!

A Bit of Background

What do a lamb, a loaf of bread, and a gate have in common? The answer is best explained in an exciting object lesson or devotion. Kids love snappy devotions built around simple objects, dynamite demonstrations, and surprising stunts. And the best part? Kids remember the messages! Short lessons and devotions involving concrete objects help kids visualize meanings. Jesus knew the value of concrete examples in his own teaching. Remember how Jesus taught us not to point out the speck in a neighbor's eye when we have a plank in our own? Ouch! We can almost feel that woody sliver and know the pain of judging others! Kids have limited vocabularies and are unable to conceptualize abstract concepts. By using concrete items and examples in devotions, you're on the way to ensuring understanding in an age-appropriate way.

Many devotions and object lessons can be led by kids. Choose a devotion, then copy it and send it home with a volunteer. Encourage the child to practice presenting the devotion to family and friends, then be ready to present it to the class the following week. When kids take an active role in presenting short devotions to their peers, they nurture a sense of responsibility for their learning and have a chance to serve and teach others.

For fun impromptu devotions, provide a variety of objects from a particular category, such as foods or items found in nature. Have children form pairs or trios, then invite each group to choose an item. Challenge the groups to design a devotion that answers the following questions:

- How does the item show God's love for us?
- How is this item like our faith in God?
- In what ways can we thank God for this item? for his love?

Have children present their devotions to another group or to the entire class.

When planning or searching for the right devotion to present, be sure to stay in tune with the theme of the Bible lesson. And remember, the greater the "wow factor," the greater the recall! Snappy devotions with surprising demonstrations are real memory-makers.

Always end object lessons and devotions with a summary sentence that keys into the object of the devotion. For example, an object lesson using a brick to illustrate strong faith might be summed up as "God helps strengthen our faith in surprising ways."

Be creative in your devotions and look for ways to add an element of surprise in object lessons. And finally, what do a lamb, a loaf of bread, and a gate have in common? They're all names for Jesus!

JOINED IN JESUS' LOVE

Sharing Jesus' love
Matthew 28:19, 20

Whatcha Need: You'll need a Bible, scissors, tape, and 8½-by-3-inch strips of paper.

Preparation: Cut two paper strips for each child, plus a few extras.

Whatcha Do: Ask children how good news can bring people together, why the news about Jesus' love is good news to us, and why we want to share the good news about Jesus with others. As children tell their ideas, give one strip of paper half a twist, then tape the ends together on both sides. Show the strip and explain that the one strip is like one person who knows the good news about Jesus. Then tell children to watch what happens when the good news is shared with someone else. Poke the scissors through the center of the strip and snip all the way around until you snip through your beginning cut. Hold the strip up and point out how one circle has become two joined circles. Explain that when we share Jesus with someone else, we become joined by his love and want to tell more people! Read aloud Matthew 28:19, 20. Ask:

Turn one end once and tape — cut

- ● **What can we tell others about Jesus?**
- ● **How does telling others about Jesus' love help them? help us? join us together?**

Hand out paper strips and teach everyone how to do this simply stunning trick. Then challenge children to share this devotion with two other people as they tell them about Jesus' love.

Whatcha Know!

Use colorful wrapping-paper strips for a festive touch. Suspend several of these joined circles from clothes hangers or plastic drinking straws for simple, yet striking, mobiles. Add cards that say, "Joined in Jesus' Love."

SINK OR SWIM

Loving Jesus on the inside
Zechariah 7:11, 12

Whatcha Need: You'll need a Bible, scissors, sponges, a glass bowl filled with water, and a small fishing sinker.

Preparation: Cut two 2-inch squares from the sponge. Use scissors or a knife to make a slit in the bottom of one sponge, then hide the sinker inside. Test the sponge in water to make sure it sinks.

Whatcha Do: Set the bowl of water on the table and the two sponge squares beside the bowl. Hold up the sponges and ask children to predict what will happen to the sponges when they're placed in water—will they sink or float? Place the sponges in the water and watch the weighted one sink to the bottom. Children will be very surprised at the outcome! Ask:

- ● **Why did you think the sponges would float?**
- ● **How did one of the sponges deceive you?**

Explain that both sponges look the same on the outside and appear to be real sponges but that one sponge is hiding a secret on the inside that makes it sink. It may look and act like a sponge on the outside—but it's not on the inside! Ask children how the sunken sponge is like someone who only loves God on the outside but not on the inside.

Then read aloud Zechariah 7:11, 12. Point out that it's important to obey God, to be teachable, and to be kind to others on the inside as well as on the outside. Remove the hidden sinker from the sponge, then wring out the water. Place the sponge back in the bowl and watch it float. Remind children that when we truly love God, we're careful to love and obey God on the inside as well as the outside!

GOD'S CONTROL
God is in control.
Ephesians 4:6

Whatcha Need: You'll need a Bible, nine markers, a paper sack, and a piece of paper.

Preparation: Tear the piece of paper into nine squares—three across the top, three across the center, and three across the bottom as in the diagram. Notice that the center piece has four ragged edges. This is the square you'll need to remember during this clever devotion.

Whatcha Do: Gather children in a group and tell them you have an amazing power that lets you read minds. Then hand nine children each a torn paper square and a marker. Remember which child you handed the square with the four ragged edges. Instruct the nine children each to write one word that describes God on their papers. They can confer with friends if they'd like.

When the words are written, have a volunteer collect the squares in a paper sack. Tell children that you'll pick one person and choose the word he wrote. Look around the group, select the child who had the square with four torn edges, and indicate you'll read his word. Reach into the sack and remove the paper squares. Read all of the words aloud, then hold up the square with the ragged edges as the correct square. The children will be amazed! Then explain that this was, of course, a slick trick and that you can't really read minds or pick out words or know what will happen tomorrow but that God can do these things. Remind children that God is all-powerful and ever-present. God knows the things we say and do, and God knows what tomorrow will bring because God is in control of everything! Then read aloud Ephesians 4:6 and ask:

- ● **How does knowing that God is in control help us?**
- ● **Why do you think God didn't give us ultimate control over the world?**

● **How does knowing that God is in control strengthen our faith? our trust?**

Show children how to do this cool trick, then challenge them to present this devotion to their friends at school and to their families.

CREATION CELEBRATION

Giving thanks
Ephesians 5:20

Whatcha Need: You'll need a Bible, clear Con-Tact paper, scissors, and white or pastel construction paper. This devotion works best outside, so plan accordingly.

Preparation: Cut a 12-inch square of clear Con-Tact paper for each child. Leave the backing on the paper.

Whatcha Do: Hand each person a square of clear Con-Tact paper. Help children carefully remove the paper backing, then hold the Con-Tact paper to the fronts of their shirts with the sticky side facing out. Fold back the top edge of the paper a bit and stick it to the shirt to keep the paper in place. Do the same at the bottom of the Con-Tact paper. Children should now be wearing sticky bibs. Then take a walk around the church or the block. Encourage children to look for unusual leaves, pretty flowers, seeds, and small twigs to stick to their paper bibs. As you walk, remind children how God made the world and all that is in it. Ask children to look for their favorite parts of creation as they walk along.

When the bibs are full, return to class and invite children to show off their wearable collages. Ask:
● **How does God's creation show his love for us?**
● **Why is it important to keep God's creation clean and beautiful?**
● **What are ways we can thank God for his loving creation?**

Read aloud Ephesians 5:20, then offer a prayer thanking God for his love and for his loving creation. Gently remove the bibs and have children turn their collages over and stick them to light-colored construction paper. (The items will show through the clear Con-Tact paper.) Then arrange the lovely collection on a church wall with the caption "Celebrate God's Creation!"

POWER PLAY

The Holy Spirit's power
Romans 15:13

Whatcha Need: You'll need a Bible, markers, curling ribbon, and balloons.

Preparation: None required.

Whatcha Do: Hand each child an uninflated balloon. Explain that you are going to have a few balloon races to see how far the balloons can travel. First have children throw their uninflated balloons as far as they can. After several tosses, instruct them to inflate the balloons but not tie them

off. Have kids hold the balloons, then let them go around the room. After several launchings, gather children and ask:

- **In which race did the balloons travel best? Why?**
- **How are balloons with air in them like having the power of the Holy Spirit inside us?**
- **In what ways does the Holy Spirit help us go farther in helping others, learning about God, and showing kindness?**

Read aloud Romans 15:13, then remind children that the Holy Spirit was sent to us after Jesus' death and resurrection to help us do the things Jesus would do if he were still here on earth. In other words, the power of the Holy Spirit inside us helps us do the things Jesus would do! Have children inflate and tie off their balloons. Help children write the words "Powered by the Holy Spirit!" on their balloons, then have children decorate their balloons with markers. Tie colorful ribbon cascades around the knot. Tell children to take their balloons home as a reminder of how the Holy Spirit empowers us to do good things for Jesus.

"DOTS" THE WAY!

God's help
Psalm 91:1, 2

Whatcha Need: You'll need a Bible, pencils with erasers, and photocopies of the dot pattern illustrated on page 82.

Preparation: Draw the dot pattern from the following page on a sheet of paper (omitting the lines). Make one photocopy of the dots for each child.

Whatcha Do: Have children form pairs or trios and hand each child a pencil and a photocopy of the dots. Challenge the children to see if they can connect all the dots with four straight lines and without lifting their pencils from the paper. Allow several minutes to work on solving this difficult puzzler, then show children how to solve it. After everyone has drawn their lines, ask:

- **How is this puzzle like having troubles or problems in our lives?**
- **In what ways can God help us solve our problems and worries?**
- **Why is trusting God important when we ask for his help?**

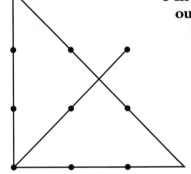

Remind children that they solved their puzzles when they followed your directions. Point out that it's important to obey God and that God can direct us to find ways to solve our toughest problems and worries if we trust him. Ask a volunteer to read aloud Psalm 91:1, 2. Then close with a prayer thanking God for his wisdom in helping us solve our worst troubles and worries.

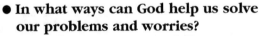

Whatcha Know!

Try making a human dot-board. Have nine children stand in the dot pattern, then have the rest of the children attempt to join the "dots" with a 30-foot-long string.

GOD'S SECRET WEAPON

Serving God
Colossians 3:23

Whatcha Need: You'll need a Bible, a decorated gift box, and a mirror.

Preparation: Wrap the box and lid separately. Place the mirror in the bottom of the gift box, with the reflective side facing up. Set the lid on the box.

Whatcha Do: Have children sit in a circle and show them the gift box. Tell children that inside the box is a secret weapon that belongs to God. Explain that this weapon is so special, there is only one like it in the entire universe! Tell children that this secret weapon can accomplish God's will and has the potential of bringing love and light to the world. Ask children to tell what they think might be inside the box, then pass the box around the circle. Let each child peek in the box at God's secret weapon but not tell anyone what's inside. When the box has been around the circle, ask children what they saw. Then ask:

- **In what ways are each of us like God's secret weapons?**
- **How can we accomplish God's will? bring light and love to the world?**
- **What are we "weapons" against?**

Explain that we are weapons against hatred, evil, prejudice, jealousy, and lies. Ask children how we can be effective weapons for God. Then point out that we don't need to be secret about serving or loving God. Read aloud Colossians 3:23, then ask children what they can each do in the coming week to serve God by bringing light and love into the world. End by passing the open box around the circle once more. Each time a child peeks inside, have her say, "I serve God in love!"

PERFECT PEANUTS

God's sees our hearts.
1 Samuel 16:7

Whatcha Need: You'll need a Bible, a bag of peanuts in the shell, Tacky craft glue, and red or pink fingernail polish or acrylic paint.

Preparation: Before class, choose a peanut and gently open it without breaking the shell. Use fingernail polish or acrylic paint to carefully paint a tiny heart on the peanut. Let the heart dry, then put the peanut back inside the shell and glue the shell together. Remember which peanut has the heart inside!

Whatcha Do: Have children form groups of four or five and hand each group five peanuts. Set the peanut with the hidden heart aside for the moment. Challenge children to look at their peanuts and choose the most perfect one from their group of five. Encourage children to decide how they'll choose a perfect peanut, for example, by color, size, shape, or whatever criteria they choose. Allow several minutes for children to make their selections. When all the perfect peanuts have been chosen, allow groups to display their peanuts and tell why each was chosen as the best. Place those peanuts with the peanut containing the hidden heart, then have children choose the best peanut from this new group.

Before opening the peanuts, ask children how they think God would choose the perfect peanut. Explain that God looks at things differently than people do.

Read aloud 1 Samuel 16:7, then ask children what God sees when he looks at us. Ask:

● **Why do you think it's good to look at a person's heart instead of how he or she looks on the outside?**

● **How does looking at the person on the inside make us less judgmental?**

Ask volunteers to carefully open the peanuts. Hold up the peanut with the heart and remind children that God looks past the outsides and right to the heart!

GIVE IT AWAY

Giving to others
2 Corinthians 9:7; Luke 21:1-4

Whatcha Need: You'll need a Bible.

Preparation: None required.

Whatcha Do: Have children sit in a circle. Encourage children to think of something they have with themselves right now that they could give to the two people beside them as an offering. These offerings could range from a piece of fuzz on clothing to a shoe or even to a smile! Encourage children to be creative. When you say, "Please give to others," have children exchange their offerings. Then ask:

● **What sorts of things did you receive?**

● **Were you pleased? Why or why not?**

● **Why did you choose to give the offerings you gave?**

● **How did giving something of little or no value feel?**

● **What kinds of things does God want us to give to others?**

Explain that often we give just to give, without really thinking and without feeling. We tend to keep what we feel is important and give away what's not very dear to us. Tell children that God wants us to cheerfully give from our hearts. Read aloud 2 Corinthians 9:7 and Luke 21:1-4, the story of the woman who gave her only two coins to God. Ask children if this woman gave from the heart and to explain their answers. Then challenge each child to tell something she could give someone in need, such as food, an article of clothing, or even a Bible. Encourage children to bring in these items next week, then donate them to a homeless shelter. End with a prayer thanking God for our ability to give to others from the love in our hearts.

MELTDOWN!

Faith in action
James 2:14-17

Whatcha Need: You'll need a Bible, a bag of small ice cubes, a watch with a second hand, and a sunny summer day. This is a wonderful devotion to use during VBS when kids are dressed in shorts and play clothes.

Preparation: None required.

Whatcha Do: Take children outside and hand each an ice cube. Tell children to place the ice cubes somewhere on the ground and count the seconds or minutes it takes to melt them. Then ask children what might be a quicker way for them to melt ice cubes. Lead children to suggest holding the ice cubes or rubbing them between their hands or over their arms or legs. Give each child an ice cube to melt by this active friction. When the ice is melted and everyone is cooled off, ask:

● **Why do ice cubes change into water faster when they're held or rubbed instead of just sitting on the ground?**

Explain that just as ice can sit frozen on the ground and not change much, so faith can be frozen and unchanging. Tell children that it takes faith in action to change our relationship with God and make it go and grow! Read aloud James 2:14-17. Point out that when we don't learn about God, help others, or trust Jesus, our faith may become frozen. The Bible tells us it's important to have faith that is active and alive. Ask:

● **In what ways can we put our faith into action?**
● **How does active faith bring us closer to God?**

End by having children sit in a circle. Pass an ice cube around the circle and, as each child rubs the ice, have him say, "Melt frozen faith; put faith into action!"

Whatcha Know!
Prepare special ice cubes made from fruit juice for a special treat to eat. Or let children melt ice cubes made with food coloring on large sheets of white paper for a cool craft idea.

SHOW YOUR LOVE!

Loving others
Matthew 22:37-40

Whatcha Need: You'll need a Bible, a men's handkerchief, tape or needle and thread, a red marker, and a 2-inch square of thin, white cotton.

Preparation: Stitch or tape a 1-inch-wide hem along one edge of the handkerchief. Leave a 1-inch gap in the hem. Draw a red heart on the small fabric square and roll the fabric tight and flat. Slide the fabric into the gap in the hem, leaving a tiny portion sticking out. Then practice this devotion several times before presenting it to children.

Whatcha Do: Gather children in a group and hold up the handkerchief. Hold the handkerchief with your fingers over the hidden fabric. Tell the children that handkerchiefs are good for blowing your nose, then make a funny pretend blowing noise into the handkerchief. Tell children that handkerchiefs are good for mopping sweat from your brow in the summer, then wipe your forehead with the handkerchief. Tell children that handkerchiefs are also good when you're sad. Dab away pretend tears, then have children tell what things make people sad and what makes sadness go away.

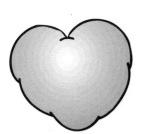

Tell children that Jesus' love makes sadness skedaddle and brings love into lives. Then read aloud Matthew 22:37-40 and ask:

● **In what ways can love help others?**
● **How does loving others show Jesus' love?**
● **Who is someone you can show your love to this week?**

Hold up the handkerchief, secretly holding the bit of fabric extending from the hem, and tell children that sad tears turn to hearts of joy (pull the fabric out and reveal the heart) when we share Jesus' love with others! If there's time, show children how to prepare their own hidden-heart handkerchiefs and challenge them to present this devotion of love to others.

JUST SAY "NO!"
Peer pressure
James 4:7

Whatcha Need: You'll need a Bible, markers, and paper.

Preparation: None required.

Whatcha Do: Gather children and ask them to tell about times when friends wanted them to do things that were wrong, such as skip a class in school, cheat on a test, or tell a lie. Hand each child three sheets of paper. Have children write the word "no" on each paper. Instruct children to fold one sheet of paper in half, then try to tear it. Ask how easy or hard it was to tear. Explain that even when we say "no" to our friends, we sometimes find it easy to break our word and "no" turns into "yes." Have children fold a second sheet of paper three times and try to tear it, then fold the last sheet of paper five times and try to tear it. Ask:
- **Why was it harder to tear the papers with many folds?**
- **How is this like saying "no" many times and not giving in?**
- **How can Jesus give us the strength to say "no" over and over again?**

Tell children that Jesus can give us the strength to say "no" to our friends even when it's difficult. Read aloud James 4:7. Point out that it's important to ask, "What would Jesus do?" If Jesus would say "no," then we can ask Jesus' help in saying "no" too! And the more times we tell our friends "no," the stronger we become—just like the strength in many folds of paper. Have children unfold one of their papers and help them write "Yes to Jesus! No to temptation!" Have children decorate the edges of their papers, then encourage children to hang their papers on a wall to remind them that Jesus gives us the strength to say "no!"

SUIT OF STRENGTH
God's armor
Ephesians 6:14-17

Whatcha Need: You'll need a Bible, balloons, clear tape, markers, and straight pins.

Preparation: Blow up and tie off two balloons. Securely stick six 3-inch pieces of clear tape on one of the balloons. Write the parts of God's armor on the pieces of tape. Refer to Ephesians 6:14-17 and include: shield of faith, breastplate of righteousness, belt of truth, gospel of peace, helmet of salvation, and sword of the Spirit. Leave the other balloon blank.

Whatcha Do: Gather children and ask them to describe a suit of armor. Have children tell what armor did for knights and warriors of long ago. Hold up the balloon without the tape and explain that the balloon represents someone who is without any protective armor. Show children the pin and encourage them to tell what will happen if the unprotected balloon is stuck. Pop the balloon with the pin, then ask:

● **How can God protect us from evil and help us resist temptation?**

Explain to children that God's love and power are like a special suit of armor we can wear every day. In fact, the Bible tells us about the armor of God. Read aloud Ephesians 6:14-17. Hold up the balloon with the tape. Read aloud the parts of God's armor, then hold up a pin. Ask children what they think will happen when we're protected with God's special armor. Poke the straight pin through the center of a piece of tape. (The balloon won't pop because the tape prevents the balloon from tearing and exploding—but don't remove the pin or the balloon may pop!) Tell children that when we know, love, and follow God, his protective armor helps us in powerful ways.

If there's time, show children how this neat trick works, then challenge them to present this devotion to their families and friends as they remind others to put on God's armor every day.

BOOMERANG BLESSINGS

Sharing
2 Corinthians 9:6-11

Whatcha Need: You'll need a Bible, paper cups, and a box of Froot Loops or other dry cereal.

Preparation: Place a handful of cereal loops in a paper cup for each child.

Whatcha Do: Hand children the paper cups of cereal. Explain that you are going to play a giveaway game. The object of the game is to try to give away all the cereal to others in 3 minutes. Tell children that players may hand one cereal loop at a time to other players but that the person receiving a cereal loop from someone can hand back two loops. After 3 minutes, call time. Ask:

● **What happened when you shared your cereal?**
● **How is this like sharing God's blessings with others?**
● **What blessings can we share with others?**
● **How do you think God feels about us sharing what we have?**

Read aloud 2 Corinthians 9:6-11. Explain that God gives each of us many blessings and that he wants us to share these blessings with others. Blessings might include food, money, clothing, wisdom, and special talents we have. Remind children that when we share with others, we not only share God's blessings, we spread God's love!

End by having children share their cereal "blessings" with the birds by tossing the cereal on the lawn for birds to enjoy. Hand each child a fresh cup of cereal to munch as you talk about times you've shared with others.

SHOW-N-TELL
Priorities
Deuteronomy 6:5

Whatcha Need: You'll need a Bible.

Preparation: None required.

Whatcha Do: Gather children in a group and tell them you're going to share some old-fashioned Show-and-Tell time. Ask children to think of one thing they have with them right now that they can show and tell the group about. Most children will probably show and tell about surface things such as articles of clothing, special jewelry, a skinned knee, or perhaps the braces on their teeth. When everyone has had a turn to show and tell, ask:

- **What do the things we've shared say about what's important in our lives?**
- **What things can we show and tell about that others may not be able to see, such as our faith?**
- **Which is more important to surround ourselves with: things and stuff or faith and God? Explain.**

Point out that God likes it when we have something new to show someone but that spiritual matters such as faith and our relationship with God are much more important to show and tell others about. Read aloud Deuteronomy 6:5. Remind children that it's important to recognize what things are truly important in our lives and that nothing is more important than knowing, loving, and obeying God!

IT'S WORTH IT!
Striving for Christ
Philippians 3:14

Whatcha Need: You'll need a Bible; paper towels; a large, clear glass of water; a 6-inch square of cardboard; a small, plastic pull-apart egg; a slip of paper; a pen; and a dishpan.

Preparation: Write the word "Jesus" on the slip of paper and place it inside the small pull-apart egg. When children arrive, have the glass of water with the egg inside inverted on a tabletop. To turn the water-filled glass upside down, simply cover the top of the glass with the cardboard square. Hold the cardboard in place and quickly invert the glass on a table. Slide the cardboard from under the glass and wipe up any excess water. You may need to try this a few times to be successful—but this devotion is worth it. (And that's what the devotion is all about!)

Whatcha Do: Set the dishpan to the side. Gather children around the upside-down glass with the egg inside. Tell children that something very valuable is inside the egg, then have them brainstorm ways of removing the egg without spilling the water. After several minutes of creative problem solving, tell kids that this is a tough problem. Explain that we often face obstacles to attaining things, but if what we're striving for is worth it, we keep trying. Ask:

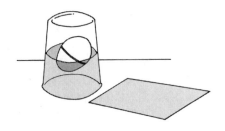

- **What things are worth striving for?**
- **Why is it important to keep trying to follow Jesus?**

Read aloud Philippians 3:14. Tell children that Jesus is the most valuable treasure we can strive for. To know, love, and follow Jesus is worth any hardship or obstacle. Then ask children to tell ways we can strive to know, love, and follow Jesus, such as through prayer or treating others kindly.

Challenge children to remove the egg from the glass of water by holding the dishpan under the edge of the table and dragging the glass to the edge. Dump the water in the dishpan and remove the egg. Let children open the egg to reveal the name of the valuable treasure worth striving for—Jesus!

BURST BUBBLES

Humility
Matthew 5:5; Philippians 2:5-11; 4:13

Whatcha Need: You'll need a Bible, a bottle of soap bubbles for each child, and a sunny day.

Preparation: None required.

Whatcha Do: Give each child a bottle of soap bubbles, then lead children outside and invite them to blow bubbles. Challenge children to see how large a bubble they can blow, how many bubbles they can blow at one time, and how small a bubble can be blown. End by having children blow a bubble that won't pop. After several minutes, gather children and ask:
- **What happens if you blow too much air into a bubble?**
- **How are bubbles similar to bragging about ourselves?**

Explain that bragging about ourselves is a lot like bubbles of hot air. Bragging about ourselves is formless and soon goes away—just as bubbles pop and disappear. Tell children that Jesus wants us to be humble. Explain that being humble or meek means not bragging or showing off or calling attention to ourselves. Being humble and meek means recognizing that Jesus is the reason we're able to do good things and help others. Tell children that it's not through us, but through Christ in us, that we're able to do good. Ask a volunteer to read aloud Matthew 5:5 and Philippians 2:5-11; 4:13. Then ask:
- **What are we promised if we're humble and meek?**
- **Why do you think people who aren't self-centered are considered special by God?**
- **How does being humble help us get along with others?**

Invite each child to blow another large bubble. Then, when the bubble bursts, have each child say, "Not by me, but by Christ in me!"

FOOD FOR THOUGHT

Jealousy
James 3:16

Whatcha Need: You'll need a Bible, a piece of paper, carrots, celery, a potato, and a candy bar. Be sure to have one food item for each child, plus a few extras. Include only one candy bar.

Preparation: None required.

Whatcha Do: Have children sit in a circle and place the food items in the center on a piece of paper. Explain that everyone will choose one item of food, then you'll go around the circle and everyone will have at least one chance to exchange her food for another one. Begin by choosing one child to pick up a food item. Continue until everyone has chosen a food. Then go around the circle and let children call on someone who has a food item they'd rather have and exchange with that person. If children are happy with what they have, they don't need to pick someone to exchange foods with. However, anyone who is chosen to exchange a food item must relinquish that food item.

Continue until everyone has had two chances to exchange his food, then ask:
- **Why did you pick the food item you chose?**
- **If you didn't end up with the food item you wanted, how do you feel?**
- **How is this game like dealing with jealousy over things someone else has?**

Explain that jealousy is what we're feeling when we want what someone else has. We might be jealous over toys, bikes, how someone looks, or the grades others receive. Read aloud James 3:16, then ask children why they think God warned us against jealousy. Talk about ways to deal with jealous feelings. Ways might include prayer, sharing, being truly kind to the person we're jealous of, and thanking God for our own blessings. End by telling children that being thankful for our own gifts and not envying others is sweet to God. Share a prayer thanking God for all you have and for helping you not be jealous of anyone or anything. Then share the candy bar and other foods!

 # FOLLOW FRIENDS
Church
Philippians 2:1-4

Whatcha Need: You'll need a Bible, paper clips, and small magnets. Refrigerator magnets will work well.

Preparation: None required.

Whatcha Do: Have children form several small groups and hand each group several paper clips and a magnet. Challenge children to try different ways of dragging all their paper clips across the table or floor. Children might drag the clips one by one, stack the paper clips, or make a paper-clip chain. After several minutes, ask:
- **Which was the best way to pull a lot of paper clips? Why?**
- **Why was it easier to move the clips in a group rather than one by one?**
- **How is this activity like people working together in a church instead of one by one?**

Tell children that the Bible refers to the church as the body of believers. When we work for God, we get things done better when we pull together as a group. Churches allow people to help each other and serve others in a bigger way. Read aloud Philippians 2:1-4, then have children discuss ways we can pull together in church to serve God. Each time a way to pull together is mentioned, add a paper clip to another one to make a chain. See if you can add one paper clip for each child in class. When the chain is complete, have everyone help hold it as you offer a prayer thanking God for your church and for the selfless people who pull together in God's name.

UNBREAKABLE TRUST

Trusting Jesus
Proverbs 3:5, 6

Whatcha Need: You'll need a Bible, paper plates, two raw eggs, markers, and damp paper towels.

Preparation: Draw a heart on one of the eggs.

Whatcha Do: Have children form a circle. Place each egg on a paper plate, then set the paper plates on the floor in front of you. Say: **One of the most fragile objects in life is an egg. The thin shell of an egg keeps the insides in but does little to protect the delicate egg from destruction. Eggs are easy to crack, simple to smash, and can't be put back together once they're broken.** Crack or smash the egg without the heart. (For a dramatic effect, break the egg in the palm of your hand.)

Say: **Trust is as delicate as an egg and as easy to break. We trust our friends to keep secrets. We trust parents and teachers to love and guide us. We trust that the sun will always rise in the east. But trust can be broken when promises aren't kept or lies are spoken. Sometimes it's hard for us to trust, but there is someone who will never break his word or destroy our trust.**

Read aloud Proverbs 3:5, 6. Then ask:

● **Why is it safe to put our trust in Jesus?**
● **How are love and trust related?**
● **Why is it important to trust in Jesus?**

Place the egg with the heart lengthwise in the palm of your hand so the ends of the egg point toward your fingers and the heel of your hand. Squeeze the egg as you talk about trusting Jesus. For example, you might say, "Even when we feel squeezed by doubts and fears, Jesus will never break our trust, and his love will keep us whole. Let's pass the egg around the circle as we thank Jesus for never breaking our trust." Show children the correct way to hold the egg so it won't break as it's being squeezed. Then have each child squeeze the egg and say, "I trust you, Jesus, and thank you for your love."

CAN'T HIDE INSIDE

Forgiveness
Psalm 86:5

Whatcha Need: You'll need a Bible, a clear drinking glass, scissors, and red and blue construction paper.

Preparation: Cut a small red heart from red construction paper. Next, trace the rim of the drinking glass on blue construction paper and cut out the circle. Tape it to the opening of the glass, being careful not to let the tape show. Place a sheet of blue construction paper on a table. Set the red heart in the center of the blue paper and turn the glass upside down over the heart. The blue paper on the rim of the glass will hide the heart without being visible itself. Practice this devotion several times before presenting it to children. Hint: Be careful to lift the glass off the blue paper only a bit so children don't see the paper taped to the rim!

Whatcha Do: Place the heart in the center of the blue paper and the glass beside it, upside down on the blue paper. Then gather children around the table. Invite children to tell about times they needed forgiveness for something they said or did. Point to the heart and explain that when we do or say things that God tells us are wrong, our hearts ache. We try to hide our hearts from God. Carefully move the glass to hide the heart, which will look as if it's disappeared. Tell children we often try to deny what we did was wrong. Ask children if we can ever hide from God.

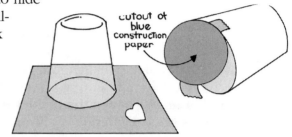

cutout of blue construction paper

Read aloud Psalm 86:5. Explain that God knows every thought and feeling in our hearts and that we can't hide from him. Then have children tell what we can do when we do or say something wrong. When someone suggests asking God's forgiveness, have each child think of one thing she could silently ask God's forgiveness for right now. Then offer a prayer asking God to forgive the wrong things we've said and done and thank him for his gift of forgiveness. After the prayer, quickly slide the glass from the heart, being careful not to lift the glass too much. Tell children that when we ask for God's forgiveness, it's as if we have new hearts filled with love!

If there's time, show children how to do this great devotion, then encourage them to share the message of God's forgiveness with their families and friends.

SUPER SEASONALS

Fanciful bulletin boards, holiday gifts, seasonal snacks, and lots more help kids celebrate the seasons in style!

A Bit of Background

What's your favorite season? The bite of chilly autumn air as it crinkles your nose or that fresh December snow, as perfect and white as any Christmas card? Maybe it's the first warm springtime breeze that sets daffodils nodding, or the tingly summer sun that turns a sandy beach into a twinkle of diamonds. Whatever your favorite time of year, seasons are one of God's most beautiful and useful gifts to us. And seasonal delights are guaranteed to fill kids with wonder, awe, and merry excitement! Make the most of this natural motivation, and plan for many seasonal activities this year. From crafts to Christmas gifts to bulletin board displays, turn your room into an inviting seasonal retreat as you celebrate God's glorious gifts.

Give your room a seasonal overhaul at the start of fall, winter, spring, and summer. Consider turning one bulletin board or wall into an ever-changing display. Cover the background with a striking blue and plan to leave it up all year for simplicity. In the fall, attach a large tree branch and invite kids to tear orange, red, yellow, and brown paper leaves. Write their names on the leaves and tape them to the branches. Or consider writing on the leaves the names of Bible characters you'll be studying in the coming year. As the months progress, alter the tree scene by adding fiberfill snow to the branches and ground in December and putting a bright star in the sky at Christmas. By the time spring rolls around, glue tissue-paper flower buds to the tree and flowers to the ground below. Be sure to attach several fluffy fiberfill clouds in the sky. You'll have a wonderful display all year with a minimum of work!

Seasonal and holiday crafts are great fun for kids of all ages! The crafts in the Super Seasonals section of this book contain unique projects that guarantee smiles all year long. Try several seasonal cooking projects and don't overlook wearable crafts that reflect the celebration of the season. T-shirts with prints of colorful autumn leaves or tie-dyed in autumn colors are as fun to make as they are to wear.

Finally, don't be as predictable as the seasons! Offer chilly winter crafts in July for a bit of cool fun. Try making frilly orange Valentine's cards in October to remind others of your love. Or put new words to familiar Christmas songs and have a unique St. Patrick's sing-along! Whatever the season, celebrate with fancy, fun, and flair as you and your kids create memories enough to last all year long!

LEAFY PRINTS

Beautiful cloths will brighten autumn tables.

Whatcha Need: You'll need tempera paints, paintbrushes, newspaper, paper plates, and a 10-inch square of white cotton fabric for each child. You'll also need a variety of leaves for each child.

Preparation: Cover a table with newspaper. Pour red, orange, yellow, and brown paint in paper plates (or Styrofoam trays) and set them on the newspaper. Place a paintbrush by each plate.

Whatcha Know!

Consider using a 3-by-5-foot length of white muslin and having your class make a printed leaf banner to hang in the church entryway. Paint "God's Season of Beauty" across the top and position colorful leaf prints over the rest of the banner. Glue gold braid along the top and bottom edges of the banner for a glittery grand finale.

Whatcha Do: Have children bring in autumn leaves or take a walk to collect different varieties. When the leaves are collected, spread a square of white fabric on the table. Demonstrate how to brush leaves on one side with paint and then press the painted sides of the leaves onto the fabric squares.

Encourage children to make unusual designs with the leaf prints, overlapping them and using a variety of colors and different-shaped leaves. As you work, visit about God's season of change and how God helps us get ready for winter. Point out that God's plan in autumn helps ready us for winter but that it is also a time of beauty to enjoy and thank him for.

When the prints are completely dry, tell children to use them as table scarves on their dining tables. Kids can set pretty flower arrangements on the scarves or place the salt and pepper shakers on them for a festive seasonal look. Encourage children to offer prayers at family meals thanking God for his time of preparation and beauty.

PRAYER CORNUCOPIAS

Thanksgiving prayers surround this creative craft.

Whatcha Need: You'll need a Bible, rubber bands, ribbon, markers, slips of paper, tape, scissors, and brown construction paper.

Preparation: Cut five 8-inch lengths of ribbon for each child. Cut a 10-inch circle from brown construction paper for each child or cut several circles from cardboard for children to use as patterns for cutting their own circles. Follow the directions in the activity to prepare a finished Prayer Cornucopia as an example.

Whatcha Do: Hold up the cornucopia and ask children if they know what you're holding. Tell children that cornucopias are often called horns of plenty, then ask children why they think that might be a good name. Explain that a cornucopia, or horn of plenty, symbolizes the bounty of autumn harvest. Read aloud Psalm 100:4; 1 Corinthians 15:57; and Hebrews 13:15, 16. Ask children why thanking God for all he gives is a good idea. Have children tell about times they thank God through prayer, such as when they say blessings before meals. Then ask volunteers to explain the significance of Thanksgiving and why this is an especially good time to thank God for all he's given us.

Tell children they'll be making Prayer Cornucopias to set on their dinner tables at Thanksgiving. Explain that these cornucopias are special because they will hold ideas to pray about with their families. Hand out the brown paper circles and have children cut halfway through the circles. Overlap the cut edges of the circle, gently pull the sides together to make a cone-shaped cornucopia, and tape the sides together. Then hand each child several slips of paper and a marker. Have children write the names of things they can thank God for, such as families, food, homes, good health, church, and Jesus. Instruct children to write one word on each slip of paper, then roll the paper into a scroll. Place rubber bands around the scrolls and tie ribbons over the rubber bands. Finally, place the prayer scrolls in the cornucopias.

 # CINNAMON LEAVES
What a delicious way to celebrate the harvest!

Whatcha Need: You'll need a Bible, flour tortillas, cinnamon sugar, a paper bag, margarine, an electric skillet, paper towels, paper plates, and a fork.

Preparation: Prepare cinnamon sugar by mixing 2 cups of granulated sugar with ¼ cup of cinnamon. Pour the cinnamon sugar into a paper bag.

Whatcha Do: Melt 2 cups of margarine in the electric skillet. Set the heat on medium high, but watch so the margarine doesn't burn. Invite children to wash their hands, then tear "leaves" from flour tortillas. As children work, discuss how God provides food for us at harvesttime and how thankful we are for our abundance. Point out that in Bible times, just as today, the harvest and God's good food have been celebrated.

When the tortilla leaves are torn, have an adult place them in the hot margarine to fry for several minutes, turning the leaves over during the cooking process. When the leaves are golden brown, drop them in the paper bag of cinnamon sugar and shake the bag to coat the leaves. Remove the cinnamon leaves and place the sweet-'n-spicy treats on paper towels to absorb any excess margarine. As you enjoy your tasty harvest, read Deuteronomy 16:13-15 to learn one way people in the Old Testament celebrated God and his abundant harvest.

> ## Whatcha Know!
>
> These delicious leaves make perky party foods. Place the edible leaves in a woven basket—it will look as though you've just raked up a basketful of colorful autumn leaves.

 # "BE-LEAFERS" IN JESUS
Enliven your classroom with this special autumn display.

Whatcha Need: You'll need a Bible, tape, markers, and a large tree branch. You'll also need red, orange, and brown construction paper and red, orange, and yellow crepe paper.

Preparation: Cover the bulletin board with brown paper (or brown paper grocery sacks). Use tape, staples, or pins to attach the tree branch to the center of the bulletin board. Add a border of twisted red, orange, and yellow crepe paper. Add a title that says, "Be-Leaf in Jesus and Be Saved!" Set the craft materials nearby.

Whatcha Do:
Gather children around the bulletin board and ask a volunteer to read aloud the title. Ask children to explain what they think this means, then read Romans 10:9. Explain that when we know, love, and follow Jesus, and when we tell others that Jesus is God's Son, we're called believers. In other words, we're believers when we believe and declare that Jesus is our Savior who died for our sins so we could be forgiven and live forever with God. Ask children:

● **Why is being a believer so wonderful?**
● **How can we help others to know, love, and follow Jesus?**
● **How does being a believer bring us closer to God? to Jesus? to each other?**

Invite children to tear construction-paper leaves and to write their names on the leaves. Hang or tape the leaves on the tree branch on the bulletin board. (Play Amy Grant's song "I Have Decided" as children work on their paper leaves.) Then challenge children to tell others about Jesus during the next several weeks. Each time they tell someone that Jesus is Lord or that they believe Jesus is God's risen Son, have them write their name or the name of the person they witnessed to on a paper leaf. See if children can fill out your "believer tree" in one month.

FRUIT OF THE SPIRIT
Play this fast-paced harvest game to review the fruit of the Spirit.

Whatcha Need:
You'll need a Bible, scissors, colored construction paper, markers, and two small baskets.

Preparation: Cut two each of the following fruits from construction paper: orange peaches, yellow lemons, brown kiwis, purple grapes, yellow pears, red strawberries, yellow grapefruit, and brown figs. Also cut out two jar shapes from orange construction paper. Write the fruit of the Spirit on the paper fruits: Love (on the lemons), Joy (on the jar shapes), Peace (on the peaches), Patience (on the pears), Kindness (on the kiwis), Goodness (on the grapes), Faithfulness (on the figs), Gentleness (on the grapefruit), and Self-control (on the strawberries). Place a set of fruit in each basket.

Whatcha Do:
To begin, read aloud Galatians 5:22, 23 to review the fruit of the Spirit. Have children describe the characteristics of each fruit, then explain you'll play a game to review the fruit. Hold up the paper fruits and read aloud the words on each. Point out that most of the fruits begin with the same letter as the corresponding fruit of the spirit—for example, the fig represents faithfulness. Explain that joy is a little tough, so kids should think of a jar of

Whatcha Know!

Use the paper fruits in a bulletin board display or keep them in a basket and pull out one fruit each week. Challenge children to look for ways to use that gift during the coming week.

their favorite fruit jam when they see that shape. Place the baskets containing the paper fruits at one end of the room, then form two groups at the opposite end. Explain that when you call out the name of a fruit of the Spirit, a child from each group is to run to find that fruit in the fruit basket. Bring the fruit back to the group and pass it to each person, who says the name, such as patience or kindness. The last person may then set the fruit on the floor. Continue in this relay style until all the fruit of the Spirit have been retrieved.

End game time with a prayer thanking God for helping us nurture each of these good traits in our lives.

STAINED-GLASS PRETZELS
Christmas ornaments or tasty treats—all in one!

Whatcha Need: You'll need large round or three-ringed pretzels, aluminum foil, cookie sheets, Tacky craft glue, yarn (if you plan to use these as ornaments), and access to an oven. You'll also need small pieces of cut-rock candy or rolls of Life Savers candies. Cut-rock candy (hard candy "wheels" with tiny designs running through them) is sold at Christmastime.

Preparation: You may wish to try this clever craft or snack idea at home before presenting it to children. If you plan to make ornaments, cut 8-inch lengths of yarn.

Whatcha Do: Preheat the oven to 300 degrees. Explain to children that they'll be making Christmas snacks (or ornaments) that will remind everyone of beautiful stained glass. Encourage children to describe the stained-glass windows they've seen, then explain that stained-glass windows often show scenes from the Bible. Artisans and craftsmen create stained-glass windows to decorate churches and, when the sun shines through the beautiful glass, we are reminded of the great light of God's love for us.

Whatcha Know!

These beautiful ornaments are fragile, so always make several extras. Place these simple—but simply lovely—ornaments on the church Christmas tree!

Hand everyone three round or ring-shaped pretzels: one to nibble and two for their ornaments or special treats. Ask volunteers to line the cookie sheets with aluminum foil as you pass six cut-rock candies or Life Savers candies to each child. Show children how to arrange their pretzels on the cookie sheet and then place one piece of hard candy in the center of each pretzel ring. Remind children to remember where on the cookie sheet they've placed their pretzels! Place the cookie sheets in the oven for about 10 minutes or until the candies have melted and filled the pretzel rings. Be careful not to burn the candies. When the candies are melted, remove the cookie sheets from the oven and let the pretzels cool for 10 minutes.

To make Christmas tree ornaments, glue yarn loops to the tops of the pretzels. For snacks, simply enjoy nibbling!

SNOW SOAP

Create snowballs with a "clean" message.

Whatcha Need: You'll need a Bible, a large bowl, water, an electric mixer, wax paper, and a box of Ivory soap flakes.

Preparation: Prepare the snowball soap mixture by mixing 4 cups of Ivory soap flakes and 1/4 cup water. Mix the soap flakes and water until they're the consistency of a stiff dough. Keep the soap mixture in an airtight container until you're ready to use it.

Whatcha Do: Gather children and talk about times they've needed to wash their hands. Explain that when our hands become dirty, it feels bad and we want to wash them. Point out that washing hands keeps them clean and free of germs that can harm us. Ask children how sin is like having unclean hands. Lead children to recognize that sin is like a deadly germ or virus that can cause us great harm—even death. Then ask children how they can wash away sin and make their lives clean again. Read aloud Psalm 51:7 and 1 John 1:7, then ask:

● **How can Jesus' forgiveness help us feel clean and new on the inside?**

● **In what ways does Jesus' forgiveness demonstrate his love for us?**

● **How can we receive Jesus' forgiveness in our lives?**

Explain that you'll be making soapy snowballs to remind everyone that Jesus' love and forgiveness can clean away our sins.

Hand each child a piece of wax paper and a small handful of soap dough. Then invite children to mold snowballs from the dough. Remind children to avoid putting their hands near their eyes. Set the soapy snowballs on wax paper to dry for several days and tell children that each time they wash with their special snowballs, they can remember how Jesus cleanses our sins white as snow.

> ## Whatcha Know!
>
> For soap-on-a-rope, tie 18-inch lengths of jute rope into loops. Mold the soapy snowballs around the rope (opposite the knot). What great Father's Day gifts these special snowballs make!

RESOLUTION SOLUTION

Make a Christ-centered New Year's resolution.

Whatcha Need: You'll need slips of construction paper, markers, tape, and a jar with a lid.

Preparation: Before class, put a label on the jar that says "Commit to Christ!"

Whatcha Do: Have children sit in a circle. Ask children to explain what New Year's resolutions are and why people make them. Explain that resolutions are promises we make to ourselves to do something we need to do. Point out that it's often hard to keep our resolutions, especially if we make too many promises. Explain that the solution to this problem is to make just one solid resolution and to center it on Jesus! Have children brainstorm possible resolutions focused on knowing, loving, and following Jesus. For example, to know Jesus better, children might resolve to read the Bible more often or to study about Jesus' life. To love Jesus more, they might resolve to tell others about him or to spread love to people in their families or communities. And to follow Jesus better, they might resolve to help others or be more forgiving.

Hand each child a slip of paper and a marker. Direct children to write their names on one side of the paper and one way they promise to know, love, or follow Jesus better during the new year. When the papers are finished, explain that keeping resolutions is often easier when we tell others what we're trying to do. Pass around the jar and have each child read aloud his resolution, then place it in the jar. When everyone has had a turn, put the lid on the jar and set it in the center of the circle. Then end with a prayer asking God to help the children keep their resolutions. Tell children that, in several months, you will open the jar and pass out the papers to see how well the resolutions are being kept.

9 ALWAYS HERE
Younger children love this midwinter marching song!

Whatcha Need: You'll need black construction paper, tape, and white crayons or chalk.

Preparation: Cut sheets of black construction paper in half. You'll need two paper halves for each child.

Whatcha Do: Gather children and ask them to describe a shadow. Explain that we can see our shadows only when there's light. Tell children that God is with us like a loving shadow but that he's with us day and night all the time! Remind children that God is with us to help and love us. Tell children that you'll teach them a new song to remind them that God is always with us but that first they need to make pretend shadows to wear.

Hand each child two paper "shadows." Invite children to use white crayons or chalk to draw or make designs on their shadows. Tape the paper shadows to the backs of the children's shoes so they trail behind them. Then sing this action song to the tune of "The Farmer in the Dell." March around the room as you sing. Be careful not to step on each other's paper shadows!

God is always here.
God is always here.
I'm not alone where e're I roam—
God is always here.

God is always near.
God is always near.
Up and down and all around—
God is always near.

God is always here.
God is always here.
March and clap and tap, tap, tap—
God is always here.

ROSIES-N-POSIES

A sweet Valentine project!

Whatcha Need: You'll need a Bible, green florists' wire and tape, scissors, green construction-tion paper, and wrapped hard candies.

Preparation: Purchase wrapped candies with twists of paper at one or both ends, such as butterscotch disks or peppermints. Check with florists or in floral departments of craft stores for florists' tape and wire. Both are green and are used for flower stems or leaves. Cut the wire into several 1-foot-long sections for each child. You may wish to make several candy flowers as samples to show children.

Whatcha Do: Invite children to describe God's love for us, then ask:
- **What would the world be like without God's love? without our love for others?**
- **Why is it important to spread our love to other people?**
- **What are some ways we can express our love for God? for our families? for other people?**

Read aloud 1 John 4:19. Remind children that we love because God first loved us and that one way to express our love for God is to spread our love to others. Then explain that you'll be making some delicious sweetheart candies to give away as expressions of love.

For each candy rose or posie, wrap one end of the florists' wire around the twisted paper end of a piece of candy. This will make the flower. Tear green construction-paper leaves and tape them to the wire stem.

Invite each child to make at least four candy flowers. Invite children to present their rosies and posies to those they love for a special Valentine's—or anytime—expression of love!

WHO'S WHO?

An interactive springtime bulletin board kids will love.

Whatcha Need: You'll need Bibles, construction paper, crepe paper, tape, yarn, markers, blue gift wrap, scissors, straight pins, and pictures of Bible characters from an old coloring book.

Preparation: Enlarge and photocopy six to eight pictures of Bible characters from an old coloring book. Include Noah, Joshua, Peter, Ruth, Daniel, and others your class has studied. Cover the bulletin board with blue gift wrap. (Gift wrap with cloud patterns works especially well!) Add a twisted crepe-paper border.

Whatcha Do: Have children form as many groups as there are Bible characters. Hand each group a paper character and invite groups to color the characters with markers and embellish them with bits of paper. You may wish to provide other craft materials such as foil, cotton balls, or sandpaper to embellish the characters. Encourage group members to talk about their particular character and the role he played in the Bible.

When the Bible characters are finished, help children tape them across the base of the bulletin board. Then have each group make a construction-paper kite. Have children write descriptions of their Bible characters on the kite shapes. Tell children to end their descriptions with the question, "Who am I?" For example, if the character is Daniel, children might write: "I wanted to keep praying to God even when I was told to stop. I spent a sleepless night with mean lions but was saved by God's angel. Who am I?" Let children use Bibles to find their information.

Children may wish to decorate the edges of their kites. Tape 3-foot-long yarn strings to the bottoms of the kites, then tape the kites across the top of the bulletin board with the strings hanging down. Let children take turns reading the riddles and pinning the kite strings to the correct Bible characters.

LION AND LAMB PUPPETS

Make reversible springtime puppets that help describe Jesus.

Whatcha Need: You'll need a Bible, cotton balls, Tacky craft glue, markers, construction paper, and one men's white sock for each child.

Preparation: You may wish to make a Lion and Lamb Puppet as a sample.

Whatcha Do: Gather children and ask them to tell the meaning of the old adage: "Spring (or March) comes in like a lion but goes out like a lamb." Explain that people use the words *lion* and *lamb* to describe the weather, but the Bible uses them to describe Jesus. Read aloud John 1:29 and Revelation 5:5, then ask:

- **Why are these good descriptive names for Jesus?**
- **What are other words that describe Jesus?**

Descriptive words for Jesus might include loving, forgiving, powerful, and eternal. Then tell children that they'll be making Lion and Lamb Puppets to remind them that Jesus is as powerful as he is tender and loving.

Hand each child a white sock. Show children how to put the puppets on their hands, then glue cotton balls up and over their fingers. The cotton balls will become the lion's mane on one side of the puppet and the sheep's fleece on the reverse side. Have children choose one side of the puppet to be the lamb and glue on small black-paper ears, noses, and eyes. Glue pointed brown or orange ears and a black nose on the lion side. Then use markers to draw the lion's whiskers and mouth.

> ## Whatcha Know!
>
> Use these reversible puppets to help tell a variety of Bible stories, including Daniel in the lions' den (Daniel 6), Psalm 23, and the parable of the Lost Sheep (Luke 15).

When the lions and lambs are finished, let children take turns using their puppets to help describe Jesus. For example, the lion puppets may "roar" strong words such as powerful, mighty, and brave. The lamb puppets may tell descriptive words such as loving, forgiving, helping, and caring.

COLORFUL PRAYERS
A rainbow of springtime thanks.

Whatcha Need: You'll need a Bible, scissors, colored construction paper, markers, tape, fishing line, and several plastic soda-pop rings. Soda-pop rings are the holders that connect six cans of soda pop.

Preparation: Cut each plastic soda-pop holder into three sets of two connected rings. You'll need two connected soda-pop rings for each child. Cut 4-by-8 inch strips of red, blue, yellow, orange, green, and purple construction paper. Cut one of each color for every child.

Whatcha Do: Ask children to describe what Noah saw in the sky after God washed the world clean with the great flood. Read aloud Genesis 9:13-17, then see if children can name the colors of the rainbow in their correct order. (Remember the acronym ROY G. BIV? It stands for the colors red, orange, yellow, green, blue, indigo, and violet.) Remind children how Noah thanked God for keeping everyone safe in the ark. Point out that Noah also thanked God for the rainbow, which was the sign of God's promise never to flood the world again. Ask children to think about things they can thank God for that begin with the same first letters as the colors in the rainbow. For example, you might suggest being thankful for rain, since the first letter in rain matches the first letter in the color red. Or kids might give thanks for the Bible, since the word Bible begins with the same letter as the color blue.

Ask children to form pairs or trios. Hand each child a marker, two soda-pop rings, and a set of colored construction-paper strips. Tell children to write on each strip something to thank God for that begins with the same letter as that color strip. Then show children how to tape the paper strips into long or wide tubes. Make sure the writing is on the outsides of the tubes. Have children tape varying lengths of fishing line to each tube and tape the ends of the fishing line to the soda-pop holders so the hanging rainbow tubes create mobiles. Finally, tape the ends of a 2-foot length of fishing line to each side of the holders, then suspend the finished mobiles from the ceiling.

EGGSTRAORDINARY EGGS
Clever Easter eggs for everyone!

Whatcha Need: You'll need Tacky craft glue, construction paper, a paper sack, paintbrushes, chenille wires, clothes hangers, a paper punch, newspaper, a dishpan of water, model car paints, and white plastic eggs.

Preparation: Purchase white plastic eggs from any craft store. They should already have holes in at least one end and are guaranteed not to break!

Whatcha Do: Spread newspapers on the floor at different ends of the room to set up two "eggstra-special" egg decorating centers. Follow the instructions for each center below.

● **Confetti Eggs**—These are perfect eggs for young children to make. Punch out piles of construction-paper dots or purchase bags of ready-made confetti. Place the colored dots in a paper sack. Have children brush their plastic eggs with Tacky craft glue, then drop the eggs in the sack and shake. Remove the eggs and set them aside to dry. (A spritz of hair spray will protect the dots from dust and moisture!)

● **Marbled Eggs**—These eggs will delight older children and adults. Set the dishpan of water on newspaper and pour in several colors of model-car paint. (The paint will float on top of the water.) Gently swirl the water and paint with a paintbrush handle to make lovely moving designs. Then hook a chenille wire into the hole in an egg. Gently dip the egg in the center of the floating paint one time in a straight down-and-up motion. Hang the eggs from clothes hangers over newspaper to dry. Simply beautiful!

 # HAND SAND-CASTING
A super snack-bowl idea!

Whatcha Need: You'll need a Bible, plaster of paris, several dishpans of wet sand, an empty coffee can, sandpaper, spoons, and a pitcher of water.

Preparation: Mix plaster of paris according to the directions on the bag. Mix the plaster in the coffee can just before casting children's hands. Plan this activity for outdoors on a sunny day.

Whatcha Do: Gather children and sing the old classic, "He's Got the Whole World in His Hands." Then read aloud Psalms 102:25 and 119:73. Remind children that God created the world and all that is in it. Ask children what it means when they sing "He's got the whole world in his hands" and what the world might be like if God didn't have everything in his control. Then explain that you will be making hand-dishes to remind everyone that the world is in God's hands.

Have children take turns placing their cupped hands, palms down, in the wet sand, pushing down to make convex prints as deep as possible. Have children remove their hands, then pour plaster of paris over the handprints, making sure that the plaster completely covers the upraised portion of the palm. Allow the plaster to harden 10 minutes, then gently lift it from the sand. Brush away any excess sand. Use sandpaper to gently sand away any stray pieces of plaster, then set the dishes aside to dry completely.

> ## Whatcha Know!
>
> After the hand bowls are dry, they can be painted, stained, or sprayed with clear shellac to make them water resistant. These unique dishes make fun gifts for grandparents!

GET GROWING!

Get going—and growing—with this special garden activity.

Whatcha Need: You'll need a Bible, a dishpan of water, scissors, flat sponges, markers, Styrofoam meat trays, and fast-growing seeds such as radishes, beans, or marigolds.

Preparation: Cut cross or heart shapes from sponges. You'll need one sponge shape for each child. Older children may wish to cut their own sponge shapes.

Whatcha Do: Gather children and ask them to tell about different signs of spring. Tell children that spring is a time when everything seems to grow and blossom. Read aloud Genesis 2:9a, then ask:

● **Who helps the seeds and flowers to grow?**
● **In what ways does God help us grow? help our faith grow?**
● **Why is it important for our faith to grow? our love?**
● **How can we keep our love for God growing? our faith?**

Then explain that you'll be making special growing gardens to remind everyone that God helps us grow in every way, every day.

Hand each child a sponge shape and a Styrofoam tray. Invite children to decorate the trays using markers. Suggest designs such as flowers, sunshine, hearts, or other decorations that remind us of God and his love. Dampen the sponge shapes in the dishpan of water and wring out any excess moisture. Place the sponges on the trays, then sprinkle seeds in the tiny sponge pores. Tell children to keep their new gardens moist by pouring water in the trays each day and keeping them in sunny windows.

RAIN TUBES

Sing a summer song of God's love.

Whatcha Need: You'll need uncooked rice, aluminum foil, markers, rubber bands, and one long cardboard tube for each child.

Preparation: Use gift-wrap tubes or make long tubes from rolled poster board by securely taping the edges together.

Whatcha Do: Distribute the long tubes and invite children to decorate them with markers. As children work, visit about the properties of rain, such as how it pours down from the heavens and helps things grow. Ask children how rain pouring down is like God's love pouring down on us from heaven. Point out that, just as rain covers plants and helps them grow, God's love covers us and helps us grow. Explain that the tubes you're making are rain tubes and that many people in places such as Africa use the tubes as rhythm instruments when they praise God.

When the tubes are decorated, have children place aluminum foil over one end of the tubes and secure the foil with rubber bands. Pour about ½ cup of uncooked rice into each tube, then place foil and rubber bands over the open ends of the tubes. Teach children the action chant below as they shake their rain tubes and praise God for his love.

God's love is raining down, *(Shake tubes in rhythm.)*
Pouring on us all— *(Shake tubes and turn around.)*
On the meek and strong and weak, *(Shake tubes softly, then loudly, then softly.)*
On the short and tall. *(Shake tubes low, then high.)*
Verse 2: God's forgiveness is raining down...
Verse 3: God's help is raining down...
Verse 4: God's power is raining down...

CO-OP HOP
Have fun in the sun with this fast-paced outdoor game.

Whatcha Need: You'll need three old bedsheets and gobs of water balloons!

Preparation: You may wish to fill about twenty water balloons before playing this game. If children are older and there's a hose, they'll enjoy filling the balloons. Tell children to wear clothes that can get wet. This is a perfect game for VBS or family picnics!

Whatcha Do: Form three groups and hand each group a bedsheet and a number of water balloons. Have each group decide who will be the tosser and who will be the catcher. The rest of the children can hold the edges of the bedsheets to make bouncy catapults. Tell children the object of this cooperative game is to toss water balloons onto the bedsheets, then catapult the balloons to catchers, who will set them on the ground. Challenge groups to see how many balloons they can cooperatively keep from exploding. Play the game several times, switching tosser and catcher roles often.

Take a breather and talk about the cooperative nature of this game and how important cooperation is for members of a church family. When you're ready for another round, form two groups: the catapulters and the catchers. See how many balloons can be caught without exploding, then switch sides. End your cooperative fun time by seeing how high balloons can be catapulted into the air and caught again before bursting!

SUNNY GLASSES
Kids go crazy for these crazy summer shades!

Whatcha Need: You'll need a Bible, Tacky craft glue, acrylic paints, small paintbrushes, fake jewels, craft feathers, and sequins. You'll also need an inexpensive pair of plastic sunglasses for each child.

Preparation: None required.

Whatcha Do: Gather children and ask what they think God sees when he looks at us. Then ask a volunteer to read aloud 1 Samuel 16:7b. Discuss the way God looks at us and how it's different from the way people look at each other. Have children tell why it's good that God sees our hearts and not just our outward appearances. Then ask:

● **What does it mean to look at someone's heart?**
● **How can we see others as God sees them?**
● **How can looking at people's hearts instead of their outward appearances help us know them better? judge them less?**

Tell children they'll be making fun sunglasses to remind them that God doesn't use special glasses to see us—he looks through his love instead! Distribute the plastic glasses and invite children to use paints, sequins, craft feathers, and phony jewels to decorate them.

When the glasses are finished, take turns modeling the new creations. Challenge children to wear their special glasses and look beyond the outside appearances of people.

STARGAZING
Review God's promise to Abraham.

Whatcha Need: You'll need a Bible, rubbing alcohol, bowls, paper towels, food coloring, Tacky craft glue, paper cups, clear shellac spray, fine-tipped felt markers, and a bag of uncooked star-shaped noodles.

Preparation: Place several drops of food coloring in a bowl, then add 2 tablespoons of rubbing alcohol. Prepare bowls of various colored dyes. Soak uncooked noodle stars in the dyes for about 2 minutes, stirring often. Then place the colored noodles on paper towels to drain and dry.

Whatcha Do: Ask children if they know how many children Abraham had. Then read aloud Genesis 15:5. Ask children how Abraham must have felt when he looked up into the starry skies and tried to count all those stars! Talk about God's promise to Abraham and the vast number of descendants God promised him. Remind children that God always keeps his promises and that Abraham and his children grew to become a whole nation of God's people, just as God had promised!

Tell children they'll be making Starry Cups to remind them of God's great promise to Abraham. Hand out the paper cups and invite children to glue the colorful star-shaped noodles to their cups (but not to the rims). When the stars are in place, show children how to use fine-tipped markers to add tiny eyes to each star. Finally, spray clear shellac on the cups for protection. After the cups dry, children can use them to drink from.

AWESOME ORGANIZATION

Clever clues, helpful hints, tons of tips, and more make this section an invaluable classroom resource!

Who can resist a hint, tip, or super shortcut to increase the fun and decrease the work? This section is loaded with clever helps to lighten your load. From the instant-crafts box to reproducible charts and checklists, you'll find something useful for every area of your classroom management. Read through these teacher-tested tips 'n hints, then go ahead and use 'em now!

 Laminate or cover file folders with clear Con-Tact paper to make instant **erasable slates.** Simply use erasable crayons or water-based markers to write on the slates, then clean them with dry paper towels or a spritz of window cleaner! Great for games, drawing Bible scenes, and writing Scripture verses.

 Scissors stay sorted with this "eggstra" special **scissors holder.** Simply tape an empty egg carton closed, then flip it upside down so the egg cups point upward. Poke the pointed ends of scissors into the egg cups, one pair of scissors per cup. Scissors handles are easy to grab—and no more snarled blades! Decorate the carton for a festive touch.

 Always running out of craft glue? Those tiny glue bottles are a nuisance to keep filled and release too much glue when kids squeeze them. Try pouring craft glue into small baby bottles and enlarging the holes in the rubber nipples a bit. The glue flows out slowly and these **glue bottles** are squeeze-proof in little hands! Add a label reading "Glue" so someone doesn't take a sip! (Non-toxic glue is harmless.)

 Clean, empty yogurt containers make colorful **crayon cups.** Sort crayons by color or by set, then keep the cups on a plastic tray to carry to tables in one trip. Keep crayon stubs in an old coffee can for craft projects!

 Got the glitter-jitters? Keep glitter in large-holed salt and pepper or grated cheese shakers to prevent spills. These easy-to-use **glitter shakers** hold more than tiny jars that empty after a few shakes. These containers are also superb for holding and dispensing colored sand. (See next idea.)

 Sand painting is a snap when you prepare inexpensive **colored sand.** Simply pour salt into a bowl and stir the salt with a stick of colored chalk. The longer you stir, the brighter the pretend sand. Use colored sand in sand paintings, rainbow sand jars, or other creative projects.

 Use fishing line as a **picture hanger** instead of yarn or string. It's more durable and almost invisible when suspended.

Keep a **music box** in your classroom as a soft-spoken attention-getter. The soft music is an effective timer when children are picking up toys or cleaning up a work area. Or give the music box a tiny wind and challenge children to quiet down and return to their seats before the music stops playing.

Large felt squares make great **sit-upons** for story time or any together time. Simply cut bulk felt into 2-foot squares and arrange them in a circle or square. Then invite each child to find a felt square to sit on. These lightweight squares also double as colorful game bases and can even be waved back and forth in time to music.

Empty 2-liter plastic milk jugs make handy-dandy **mailboxes** when connected with clear packing tape. Simply cut away ⅓ of a milk jug at the spout end. Stack and tape the milk jugs in any configuration according to the number of children in your room. For twenty-five kids, stack and tape milk jugs five across and five tall. Decorate the plastic containers with acrylic paint pens, permanent markers, or stickers. Then hang name tags on the edge of each mailbox.

Individual chalkboards can be made from small shoe boxes. Simply cover the base of each box with Con-Tact paper, then paint the top of the lid with chalkboard paint, which is available at most building centers. Paint two coats on the lid and allow to dry for at least 24 hours. Store chalk, a felt square (eraser), and a small sponge inside the box. This is a great from-me-to-you gift idea for the kids in your class! For even more fun, cover the bottom of each box with felt. Invite kids to cut out felt shapes to use on their mini flannel boards. Store the felt pieces in envelopes inside the boxes.

How to keep young children safe and side-by-side during walks? Make **walk-alongs** by cutting plastic six-pack soda-pop holders into sets of three. Have partners each hold one of the plastic rings as they walk along. Tie colorful ribbons, with jingle bells knotted in them, to the ends of the holders to make them even more fun for young children.

Want display or **bulletin board letters** that will last a lifetime? Purchase fabric that has alphabet letters printed on it. Make sure the letters are large enough to cut out. Cut the fabric into squares that contain the letters you desire, laminate the fabric, then cut out the letters and attach them to your display. Try arranging the letters so they're not always in a straight line. This effect adds eye appeal and interest to even the plainest of displays.

Bulletin board borders come alive when they're three-dimensional. Tape small inflated balloons around the edges for a festive look or loosely twist several colors of crepe paper together for a snappy border. Other ideas include stick-on bows, crumpled paper, men's neckties, and artificial vines.

Stuck in a rut using the same paper backgrounds for your **bulletin boards?** Try using rolled cork, wallpaper, wrapping paper, aluminum foil, burlap, fabric, newspaper, maps, window shades, shower curtains, or paneling for exciting background appeal. Different colors and textures will invite children to take a second look!

Along the same lines, consider **laminating fabric** shapes, animals, or numbers to use in displays and bulletin boards. Fabric does laminate well as long as it's cotton and contains no staples or other raised rough spots. Laminated shapes are simply super and wildly colorful!

Want **finger paint** in a snap? Pour a bit of liquid starch on a plastic tray, table, or glossy-coated paper. Then sprinkle a bit of powdered tempera paint on the starch. Mix the paint and starch for smooth washable finger paints. Add a few drops of liquid dish-washing soap to make the paint even more washable!

Add a bit of vanilla, a few drops of perfume, or a dash of cinnamon to your favorite recipes for modeling dough. **Sensory modeling dough** is a delight to young noses!

Children enjoy making their own Bible **color-by-number** pages to trade with others. Simply hand each child a page from a coloring book and let her designate a coloring key for each large shape in the picture. For example, choose memory verses you've been working on and let children write the words to one of the verses inside the shapes on their coloring pages. Have children write color-coded keys and sign their names at the tops of the pages. Photocopy the pages and assemble them into a book. Hand a coloring book to each child to complete on rainy days, long trips, and during wiggle-times in adult church!

Textured finger paint can be made by adding sand or sawdust to the finger-paint recipe above. This paint looks tactile and intriguing when used on wood, paneling, or cork.

Like the instant crafts box from page 8? Then prepare an instant **games box** and be ready any time kids need to get the wiggles out! With these easy-to-find items and your imagination, you'll be able to play dozens of games in a flash. Be sure to invite your kids to create a collection of their own clever games to play. In a large box, collect the following game items:

- Ping-Pong balls
- several beanbags
- a foam ball
- a whistle
- an oven timer
- chalk
- a playground ball

- several scarves or bandannas
- a couple of jump ropes
- a bag of balloons
- masking tape (for playing lines)
- several flying rings or margarine lids
- a bag of cotton balls
- a set of plastic cups (to catch things in)

Decorate a special **gift pack** to hold tiny gifts that help celebrate birthdays and special accomplishments. Include some of these items in your gift pack: small erasers, notepads, small bags of raisins, combs, pocket mirrors, key chains, pencils, buttons, cute magnets, tiny cars or animals, shiny dimes, crayons, and pencil sharpeners. Invite children to choose a gift on their birthdays, but be sure each child has a turn!

Make several photocopies of the following **checklists,** charts, and forms. Keep them in folders and pull them out to use in an instant.

SHOPPING SUPPLY LIST

Classroom Supplies

❏ chalk
❏ construction paper
❏ crayons
❏ drawing paper
❏ glue or paste
❏ markers

❏ newsprint
❏ paintbrushes
❏ paints
❏ pencils
❏ scissors

Party Supplies

❏ balloons
❏ crepe paper
❏ decorations

_____
_____
_____
_____

❏ favors
❏ flatware
❏ invitations
❏ napkins

❏ paper cups
❏ paper plates
❏ paper towels

Food Items

_____
_____
_____
_____

Miscellaneous Items

_____
_____
_____
_____

CLASS LIST

YEAR: _____

LEADER: _____   PHONE: _____

Child's name	Address	Phone	Birthday	Parent/Guardian

PERMISSION SLIP

_____ has my permission to go

_____

_____

on _____.
        (date)

Signed: _____ Date: _____
                        (Parent/Guardian)

- -

YOU'RE INVITED!

Please come to _____!

WHEN: _____

WHERE: _____

FROM: _____

Hope to see you then!

SOS
FOR THE
SUBSTITUTE

Safe (and sane!) activities for substitute teachers and spur-of-the moment volunteers.

A Bit of Background

Few things in life are as rare to find and as difficult to keep as substitute teachers! Every children's worker and leader knows the frustration of trying to find someone to take his place in the event of illness or conflicting schedules. And the more last minute the search is, the more frustrating it becomes. But not any longer! After creating the SOS folder included in this section, you'll have substitutes who are confident and willing to take over your class. Bright activities, motivating fun, and solid learning are an instant feature of the SOS folder, which keeps any substitute leader ready to go. Simply follow the instructions in this section to assemble your folder. Then keep the folder handy for those times when you need help—and a helping hand! Use these terrific tips to make your SOS folder even more effective:

Call several people who might be interested in standing in for you in your absence. Show them the assembled SOS folder and how it works. They'll be amazed at your preparation and organization—and feel confident there will be plenty of material to keep everyone happy and learning.

Store your SOS folder in a handy spot and show several of your children where the folder is kept. This way, the children can direct the substitute leader to the folder in case of an emergency.

Change the elements in your folder often to keep the materials new and stimulating. Slide in a new Bible storybook, create your own activity or coloring pages, add new riddle and Bible-trivia cards, or insert a couple of fresh game ideas. Remember: If a substitute has already used the materials in the folder, she might be stuck!

Keep a copy of this book beside the SOS folder in the event your substitute needs another quick idea! He will find an idea to use during any part of the day while keeping kids going and growing.

Be sure to send your substitute a note of thanks after her visit! An expression of kindness and gratitude is always appreciated and might keep your substitute coming back for more!

CONTENTS OF THE SOS FOLDER

- ❑ class list
- ❑ Bible-trivia cards
- ❑ Bible riddles
- ❑ 2 reproducible coloring pages
- ❑ 2 reproducible Scripture puzzles

- ❑ 1 or 2 Bible storybooks
- ❑ Quick Games page
- ❑ Quick Crafts page
- ❑ general information page
- ❑ schedule page

SUPPLIES FOR THE SOS FOLDER

You'll need a solid-colored file folder with pockets, construction paper, markers, several small envelopes, tape, a Bible coloring book and puzzle book, small Bible storybooks, and the photocopies listed in the directions that follow.

ASSEMBLY DIRECTIONS

1. Photocopy the **Class List** from page 97. Fill in the information, then highlight the names of several children you feel would be helpful to a substitute leader. Be sure to indicate on the list what the highlighted names signify. Staple the Class List to the top edge of the folder front.

2. Make a photocopy of the **Our Schedule** from page 103. Fill in the blanks in general categories such as Bible-story time, devotion time, games, craft idea, snacks, or prayer time. (If you plan to use snack time, be sure to leave a bag of cookies or crackers with the SOS folder!) Staple this page over the Class List on the front cover.

3. Photocopy on colored paper the **Bible-Trivia** cards and the **Bible Riddles** from page 104. Cut the cards apart and store them in separate small envelopes. Label the envelopes "Bible-Trivia Cards" and "Bible Riddles." Tape the envelopes, open sides facing out, to the fronts of the inside pockets, as in the illustration.

4. Place thin-bound Bible **storybooks** in the pocket on the left side. Be sure the books are small and thin so they'll neatly fit into the folder.

5. Make one photocopy each of two **pictures** from a Bible coloring book. Turn these pages into color-by-numbers pages by numbering the coloring spaces and adding a color-coded key on the page. Use these as master copies with notes to "Photocopy as needed." You may wish to run off one set to keep in the folder. Do the same for two pages from a **Scripture puzzle** book. Keep the original books and add new pages to the SOS folder often. Place these master pages in the pocket on the right side of the folder.

6. Make one photocopy of the **Quick Games** from page 105 and one of the **Quick Crafts** from page 106. Keep these two pages in the right hand pocket of the folder.

7. Photocopy the **general information sheet** from page 107. Fill out the information and draw a simple map indicating the fire escape route you'd take for your class. Staple this page to the back cover of the folder.

folder interior

JOKES   TRIVIA

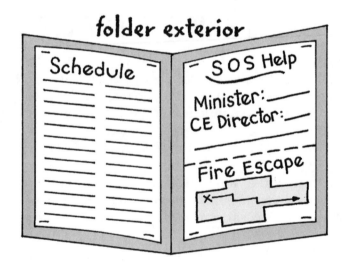

folder exterior

Schedule

SOS Help

Minister:_____
CE Director:_____

Fire Escape

Our Schedule

FROM (time)	TO (time)	ACTIVITY/LESSON

BIBLE-TRIVIA CARDS

Who was the oldest person in the Bible? How old was he? (Methuselah; 969 years old)	**What did John the Baptist eat while he was in the desert?** (locusts and honey)	**Who closed the door of the ark?** (God)	**Name three Bible women and what roles they played.** (Mary, mother of Jesus; Ruth, Naomi's friend; Deborah, judge—accept any other correct answers)
List the four books of the Bible starting with the letter M. (Micah, Malachi, Matthew, Mark)	**Where did Jesus pray on the night of his arrest? What does this garden's name mean?** (Gethsemane; olive press)	**How long did it rain when Noah was in the ark?** (40 days and 40 nights)	**What's the shortest Scripture verse in the Bible?** ("Jesus wept." John 11:35)
Who carried the rams' horns at Jericho? How many horns were there? (the priests; seven)	**How many books are in the Bible? in the Old Testament? New Testament?** (66; 39; 27)	**Name the city where Jesus and his disciples shared the Last Supper.** (Jerusalem)	**Name Jesus' twelve disciples.** (Andrew, Bartholomew, Peter, James, John, Thaddaeus, Matthew, James, Thomas, Philip, Simon, Judas)

BIBLE RIDDLES

What fish wishes it could go to Sunday school? (a holy mackerel)	**What person in the Bible had a whale of a time obeying God?** (Jonah)	**If it rained on the ark 40 days and 40 nights, how many hours was that?** (960 hours)	**What does God give away yet always keep?** (his promises!)
In Bible times, if 60 minas equaled 1 talent, how much were 10 talents worth? (600)	**How many Israelites swam across the Red Sea with Moses?** (none—they walked)	**What did the Hebrews use that grew shorter the longer they stood?** (candles)	**Which two people in the Bible never had grandparents?** (Adam and Eve!)
What has teeth but no mouth? Hint: Moses used one for his hair! (a comb)	**What did Paul walk on but never across?** (his feet!)	**What's black and white and read all over?** (the Bible!)	**Which animals on the ark liked arithmetic?** (rabbits—they liked to multiply)

QUICK GAMES

Word Safari—Hand each pair of kids a sheet of paper and a pencil. Write the word "Methuselah" on the chalkboard. Challenge pairs to see how many words they can make from the letters in Methuselah in 10 minutes. Some suggestions might include met, use, seem, mesh, and sleuth.

Recall Ball—Wad four sheets of paper to make four balls. Have kids form four groups and each group stand in a circle holding a ball. Within each group, toss the ball to one player, who says his name aloud. Then have that person toss the ball to someone else, who says her name. Remember the order you toss the ball in! Keep tossing the ball in the same order, but going faster and faster. When children have gone around the circle five times without a miss, have them try two balls or join another group to make a larger circle.

Ark-Lark—Wad a sheet of paper to make a ball. Have children sit in a circle. Begin by saying, "I'm riding on the ark with a (name of an animal)." Name an animal, then toss the ball to another person in the circle. That person repeats the sentence so far, then adds her own animal. See if you can get all the way around the circle without forgetting any animals!

Bible Scavenger Hunt—Have children form groups of two or three. Give each group a Bible. Write on the chalkboard the name of a person, a place, an event, and an object (such as an animal or a food) from the Bible. Then challenge kids to find in the Bible one from each category. As soon as a category is found, that group shouts "person!" or "place!" or whatever category has been located, then reads aloud the passage. That group scores 1 point. Continue playing until one group has accumulated 5 points.

QUICK CRAFTS

Praise Paintings—Hand each child a sheet of white paper. Place several drops of tempera paint or food coloring on the paper. Have children gently blow the drops around the paper with straws. (Don't blow too hard, or you'll splatter the paint!) When the paint dries, use fine-tipped markers to write various words to praise God over the blotches. Use words such as power, joy, love, awesome, and mighty.

Chatter Cups—Hand each child a Styrofoam cup and plastic drinking straw. Invite children to decorate the cups using markers or by gluing on bits of colored construction paper. Turn the cups upside down and poke the straws through the bottoms of the cups. When the straws are gently pushed up and down, they'll make soft squeaky noises. Use your squeaky instruments to help sing a song.

Easy Batik—Hand each child a sheet of white construction paper. Have children crumple and uncrumple their papers five times to put creases in the paper and soften the fibers. Paint the papers with watercolor paints or thinned tempera paints. The paint should be darker in the crease lines and give the pictures a tie-dyed look.

Perky Spoon Puppets—Hand each child a plastic spoon. Have children use markers to make faces on the convex (rounded) sides of the spoon. Glue on bits of construction paper or cotton balls for hair and beards. Hand a tissue to each child. Poke a hole in the center of the tissue with the handle of the puppet and slide the tissue up to the spoon head. Tape the tissue in place as a robe. Use markers to color the robes if you'd like. Then use your perky puppets to help tell favorite Bible stories!

GENERAL INFORMATION

Minister: _____

Other Leader: _____

CE Director: _____

Other helpful information: _____

_____

_____

_____

FIRE ESCAPE ROUTE

ACTIVITY INDEX

CREATIVE CRAFTS

GREAT GAMES

GOODIES GALORE

PRAYER & WORSHIP

DEVOTIONS & OBJECT LESSONS

SUPER SEASONALS